COLLINS COUNTRYSIDE SERIES
WOODLANDS

These books are intended to offer the beginner a modern introduction to British natural history. Written by experienced field workers who are also successful teachers, they assume no previous training and are carefully illustrated. It is hoped that they will help to spread understanding and love of our wild plant and animal life, and the desire to conserve it for the future.

COLLINS COUNTRYSIDE SERIES

WOODLANDS

*

William Condry

COLLINS
ST JAMES'S PLACE, LONDON

William Collins Sons & Co Ltd
London · Glasgow · Sydney · Auckland
Toronto · Johannesburg

TO ALL WHO CARE
ABOUT OUR
NATIVE WOODLANDS

First published 1974
© William Condry, 1974

ISBN 0 00 212172 7

Made and Printed in Great Britain by
William Collins Sons & Co Ltd Glasgow

CONTENTS

PHOTOGRAPHS

PREFACE

BRITAIN is but sparsely forested and we British, because nine out of ten of us live in urban surroundings, are far from being forest-minded. But in these leisured and motoring days when the farthermost depths of the countryside are reachable in a few hours, more and more of us are discovering the delights of well wooded country. We enjoy the beauty of trees, the quiet of the forest, its coolness in summer, its shelter in winter, the freedom to walk along forest rides where there are no petrol fumes or noise of engines. Perhaps too in going to the woods we are making a return journey: we are going back to the forgotten world of our ancestors who, until the end of the Dark Ages, nearly all lived near enough to primal forest for it to have been the ever-present background of their lives.

The oftener we go to the woods the more we become aware what fascinating places they are. And we ask what a woodland really is, how it got there, how long it has been there, how long it is likely to remain, what its trees are, why those trees are there and not others, what animals and birds live there, what flowers and fungi grow there, and a thousand other questions.

It is for inquiring woodland visitors that I have written this book in the hope that they may get added pleasure out of their forest-going. I would like to think too that something of what I have said may help to enlist support for the conservation of what is left of our native woodlands, for they are threatened on all sides. The destruction of these woodlands, continuous ever since Neolithic times, has now brought us to the point where we are left with the very last fragments. And these, because genuinely precious, deserve to be treated with due respect and care.

I have pleasure in acknowledging the help of experts who have written so well on forests, trees and their natural history. Their works are listed in the bibliography. I am grateful for particular help from E. H. Chater formerly of the Botany Department of the University College of Wales, Aberystwyth who has steered me round stumps of ignorance over which I would otherwise have tripped as I found my way through the various types of forest. (If I have fallen over other snags it is my own fault.) Basil Fox, Curator of the University College Botany Gardens, Aberystwyth, has patiently answered my all-too-frequent questions. So too have Gordon Mill of Machynlleth and Raymond Perry of Dolgellau, both of whom truly are men of the woodlands.

CHAPTER I

OUR WOODLAND STORY

THE fascinating story of our woodlands begins about ten thousand years ago when our climate started to warm up after the Great Ice Age. Till then life had been impossible for most forms of life because sheets of ice, sometimes immensely thick, had lain over almost the whole of the British Isles and the seas around. Why did the climate warm up? This is a question no one knows the answer to but perhaps we shall find out some day. What we can be sure about is that in those days Britain was joined to the Continent by a low-lying reach of country now lost under the southern part of the North Sea. We know this because ships dredging in the North Sea have often brought up the relics of ancient forests from the sea bed; and with them primitive weapons of wood, flint and bone that were used for fishing and hunting by prehistoric men of the Middle Stone Age. You can see for yourself the remnants of such ancient drowned forests at various places round the British coast – the stumps of prehistoric trees sticking up in the sand at low tide. Inquire at museums in seaside towns to find out whether there are any such remains to be seen nearby.

So we can picture Britain ten thousand years ago as part of the Continent and with the ice sheet gradually retreating towards the north as summers very slowly became warmer and winters less severe. The most important result of this change was that plants and trees were now able to move north from the southern parts of Europe which had not been covered by ice. Lichens, among the hardiest of all living things, were already here and now they were joined by mosses and other low-growing plants such as bilberry, cowberry and stunted bushes of birch and willow such as exist today along the northern fringe of the Arctic forests and which we call tundra vegetation. ('Tundra' is a Lapp word meaning the barren waste lands beyond the most northerly forests.)

The first real trees (as distinct from stunted bushes) to advance north were the hardy birches and pines and when they came into Britain they spread right across England, Wales, Scotland and Ireland, for Ireland in those days was joined to the British mainland. Probably all the drier ground, except high mountains, was eventually covered by forests of pine, mixed with birch; and tracts of low ground left waterlogged by melting ice sheets were colonised by willows.

By about 9000 BC the last of the permanent ice had gone altogether from Britain and perhaps by 7000 BC the ever improving climate was warm enough to allow hazel to advance here from the southern part of the Continent. After the hazel came oak, elm, lime, alder; and later ash, beech and hornbeam. Of these oak, ash and hazel have been extremely successful ever since; wych elm and alder are widespread but less abundant; but beech, lime, common elm and hornbeam have not got very far into Britain in any great quantity without the aid of man. The result is that the commonest native trees widespread in Britain to-day are oak, ash, birch, willow and alder. Of the once vast native pine forests only a few fragments survive and they are in Scotland. Beech forest, though introduced to many places in Britain, is native only in parts of south England and south Wales.

You may wonder how we can seem so sure about what happened to the forests of prehistory. The answer lies in the wonderful preserving powers of peat. But what is peat? When freshly dug out of a bog, peat is a black, soggy substance heavy with water. But when dry it becomes brown and light in weight and you can crumble it in your hands. It burns well and has always been used for fuel in districts where it is abundant. Peat consists of an accumulation of partly decomposed plant remains. Usually these are water plants such as reeds, sedges or bog moss which, when they die, cannot rot completely away because in the cold, waterlogged swamps in which they grow there is very little oxygen; and oxygen is essential to the production of complete decay. So in stagnant, airless morasses in cool, wet districts the plant remains gradually pack down layer upon layer until after many centuries there may form a twenty or thirty foot depth of peat.

Because peat does not rot away, anything that happens to get buried in it is also protected from decay. If you bury a dead animal in ordinary soil it soon decomposes. But if you buried it deep in a peat bog it might be preserved for ages. In fact the bodies of men who died in peat bogs over a thousand years ago have occasionally been recovered complete with their skin, their hair and even their clothing.

For the student of forest history what is exciting about peat is that in it is preserved the pollen blown by the wind into prehistoric swamps from trees that lived thousands of years ago. Nearly all our forest trees are wind-pollinated which means that the pollen is carried by the breeze from the male to the female flowers. So in spring when the trees are in flower great numbers of microscopic grains of pollen float about in the air. Comparatively few of these ever blow on to a female flower and fertilise it. Most are wasted, eventually falling to the ground where they rot away. But the pollen which happens to fall on to the surface of a bog may sink into the peat and so get preserved. The fact that each pollen grain is enclosed in a waterproof skin also helps it to resist decay.

Spring after spring for thousands of years the trees of prehistory spread their pollen on to the bogs of those days. As the peat built up so the pollen of the earliest forests got buried deeper and deeper, that of the later forests being laid above them. So a peat bog to-day, provided it has not been cut into for fuel or any other reason, may contain a whole sequence of tree pollen exactly in the order in which it has been laid down since trees first arrived in Britain after the Great Ice Age.

Now all this ancient pollen would be of little interest to us if it were not for one vital fact: that the pollen of one kind of tree is different in size and shape from that of another. With the aid of a microscope an expert can usually say what sort of a tree any speck of pollen came from. So the botanist who wants to investigate the history of our forests goes to a deep peat bog and bores down into it with a metal tube several metres long. When pulled up this tube contains a cross-section of the peat from the surface right down to the bottom of the bog. The botanist then takes this peat back to his laboratory and examines it for pollen grains as carefully as a detective looking for fingerprints. The sort of thing he might find is that the tree pollen near the bottom of the bog is mostly of pine, willow and birch; that in the middle depths there is, in addition, a lot of hazel and a little oak, elm, ash and alder; and that in the higher levels there is far less pine and birch and much more oak, alder and other trees. So the story of the forests of ancient times has been put together.

Such an enormous amount of water went to form the ice sheets of the Great Ice Age that when the climate was at its coldest the level of the oceans was probably one hundred metres lower than to-day. So it is understandable that the water drained right out of shallow parts of the ocean such as the North Sea and the narrow parts of the English Channel, leaving Britain joined to the Continent. When the melting ice cap returned its water to the oceans the sea-level began to rise and eventually it returned to the North Sea and the Channel, and Britain became an island. By that time (about 5000 BC) all the native trees we are familiar with had reached Britain though they were not then distributed as they are now. For instance all over the country there was at first far more pine than oak, for pine enjoyed the dry climate that lasted during the two thousand years of what is called the Boreal Period (about 7000 BC to about 5000 BC).

Somewhere about the time that Britain was separated from the Continent, the climate changed. It remained mild but became wetter and is called the Atlantic Period. These wetter conditions greatly helped oak and alder and discouraged pine. The result was that, except in swampy places, oak gradually became the common forest tree of Britain and since the climate to-day is not greatly different from what it was in 5000 BC, the oak is still the commonest of our native trees. In north Scotland there are small natural forests of pine but they are only relics of a bygone age.

Where, you may wonder, does man fit in to all these changes of climate and forest? The answer is that men had been in Britain for a vast period of time before Britain became an island. But they were in very small numbers, surviving the terrible winters of the Great Ice Age by living deep in limestone caves. They lived very primitively by hunting and by collecting wild foods. We call their period the Old Stone Age. This was followed by the Middle Stone Age when, in the warmer climate of the Boreal Period, man gradually increased in number and became less primitive but still lived as a woodland creature hunting animals and gathering fruits and roots. It was not until long after Britain had become an island that man at last reached the vital turning point in his development when he ceased to be a wandering hunter and became for the first time a cultivator. This important change came during the New Stone Age and was introduced by new races of people coming across the sea from the Continent about 3000 BC.

These new people, Britain's first farmers, brought with them cattle, sheep and seed corn. They needed fields and, being energetic and inventive, they soon found ways of making large clearings in the forests by means of fire and cleverly made stone axes with wooden handles. (You can see these beautifully fashioned blades in any good museum.) So the first attack on the forests began. Perhaps only the smaller trees were actually felled, the giant oaks being merely killed by cutting a ring into their trunks. The trees would then stand leafless in summer and

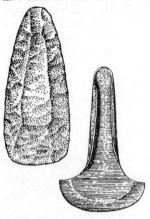

Left, late Stone Age flint axe; *right,* Bronze Age axe. With such tools man began the clearance of primeval forests

cast so little shade that it would be possible to cultivate crops quite close to them. Around New Stone Age man's little fields of corn, his grazing animals foraged among the trees eating grass and other herbage. They also ate every seedling tree they could find. So no young trees grew up to take the place of those that had been destroyed. As men increased so did their animals also; and so did their clearings in the forest.

After 2000 BC the New Stone Age was declining. Fresh peoples began to come across the sea from the Continent and with them they brought the first knowledge of the use of metal, a metal which could be made into tools and weapons that were far superior to anything that could be made from stone. This first metal was bronze which was cleverly made by mixing about nine parts of copper with one part of tin. Though copper and tin separately are both soft metals, bronze is much harder, and its invention, which was made in some eastern Mediterranean country, brought very great changes for it meant that man could now have better axes and could clear the forests at the speed he needed in order to make space for his ever-increasing flocks, herds and cornfields. It is thought that by the end of the Bronze Age all the hills of southern England we now call the downs had been cleared of trees and become grassland. It is also probable that a change of climate helped to clear those high forests: for the Bronze Age had a drier climate than the Atlantic Period and the downs probably became less suitable for tree growth.

The use of bronze for tool-making lasted until knowledge of an even better metal arrived about 500 BC when the Iron Age began. By now the climate was again becoming wetter and the oak forests were growing more vigorously than in the Bronze Age. But with the coming of iron axes to fell the trees and iron ploughs to turn the ever-increasing forest clearings into cultivated fields, the forests continued to retreat. In the Iron Age really big areas of southern England came under cultivation for the first time. By Roman times practically all Salisbury Plain in Wiltshire, and the nearby uplands of Dorset, were under plough; and though these districts are now covered by grass you can clearly see the earth banks called 'lynchets' which marked the outlines of those ancient fields.

All through the Dark Ages, with the population steadily increasing and giving rise to a need of more farming land, the forests continued to be attacked. Both Saxons and Danes were vigorous cultivators and they were able to tackle the great dense forests of the lowlands. So, in the course of time, they established their farms in valley bottoms whose soils had been enriched by the fertility of thousands of years of oak woodland. And once the valleys were under cultivation the earlier ploughlands on the hills were no longer needed. But they did not go back to forest; instead they became pastures for the farmers' flocks and herds. It is probable that by the time of the Domesday survey (1086) four-fifths of British forests had gone and what was left was nothing more than patches of woodland among fields – a pattern similar to to-day's, except that now there is even less woodland.

By the Middle Ages the only sizeable areas of woodland were those which the kings had protected as royal hunting forests, but by Tudor times even these had greatly shrunk. At last the country began to feel the pinch of a timber shortage. Wood, especially oak, was in great demand for houses, furniture, bridges and all kinds of ships. In the seventeenth century John Evelyn, a court official, wrote a now classic book called *Silva, or a Discourse of Forest Trees* whose message can be summed up by the single sentence: 'We had better be without gold than without timber.' Those were days when the British navy was becoming a force in the world and huge amounts of top-quality, large-sized oak were needed to build the ships. In quest of these great oaks timber merchants were having to go farther and farther afield to places long journeys away from the shipyards.

Other industries too were eager for wood: the glassmakers and the metal-smelters needed great quantities of it to keep their furnaces going. The growing iron industry wanted most of all. Already in Evelyn's day iron furnaces were springing up in thickly wooded districts of Britain. The fuel they used was charcoal which burns with twice the heat of burning wood. The trees were felled, chopped up and reduced to charcoal by burning the wood slowly with limited access to air. When the woodland of a whole district had been consumed the furnaces were rebuilt elsewhere. Perhaps our woodlands would have disappeared altogether if it had not been for the discovery of coke, which was a much better fuel for the furnaces. So in the eighteenth century the iron, lead and copper industries migrated to the coalfields, leaving the last forest fragments to survive.

The eighteenth century was also a time of other great changes in the landscape. Till then very little of the British countryside was enclosed by permanent fences as it is to-day. But in the eighteenth century former vast areas of common land were enclosed by powerful landowners and turned into farms which, because of new farming techniques then being introduced, brought the landowners considerable wealth. This increase in prosperity enabled many landowners to do what John Evelyn had urged – create new forests. So the more fertile lands were devoted to the new, intensive agriculture, and the less fertile parts such as hillsides and land with thin soils were turned into forestry plantations of both

PLATE I. Conifers native and planted. *Above,* well-spaced native Scots pines with juniper, birch and heather in Strath Spey, Scotland. *Below,* the unnaturally close trees, forced upwards to reach the light, of a conifer plantation in south England.

PLATE 2. Three woodland types. *Above left*, beechwoods are most characteristic of chalk country in southern England. *Right*, silver birch, distinguished at a distance from downy birch by its gleaming white trunk. Both birches are ready colonisers of acid soils such as sands and peats. *Left*, oakwoods like this, with well-developed field and shrub layers, are most typical of fertile clays.

deciduous and coniferous trees. This process continued well into the nineteenth century and resulted in a considerable increase in the woodland area of Britain. In south Britain, oak and beech, and in Scotland larch, Scots pine and Norway spruce, were the trees mostly used.

In the second half of the nineteenth century there was little enthusiasm for tree-planting mainly because there were now many growing industries in which landowners could invest their money and get better and quicker profits than they could ever expect from forestry. Also, much timber was being imported from abroad, causing home-grown timber to be less in demand. The result was that many British woodlands, especially the deciduous ones, fell into neglect and became more valued as coverts for pheasants and foxes than for their timber. Probably they would be in a similar state to-day had not two world wars this century used up a huge amount of timber from those woodlands, making it necessary to create new plantations which are still being added to.

When you realise that the forest area of to-day is only about one twentieth of that of the New Stone Age you will easily see that the British Isles, as a home for wildlife, has changed enormously in the past five thousand years. To take just one aspect of nature let us consider a few birds. We can be pretty sure that typical woodland species such as nuthatch, tree creeper, nightingale, woodcock and the spotted woodpeckers, if they were present in our prehistoric forests, were much commoner than they are to-day. It is possible that the hawfinch too was more abundant in the days when forests of oak and hornbeam – now its favourite Continental habitat – were larger. Other birds of the ancient forest, instead of decreasing as the forest decreased, adapted themselves to the new pattern of fields, hedges, copses, gardens and houses that took the place of the forest. This they have done so thoroughly that we can assume they are far commoner now than when they were purely woodland birds. Among these successful birds are probably robin, blackbird, song thrush and mistle thrush. Then there are other species which greatly benefited from the change from forest to cultivation, especially the seed-eaters. Birds such as chaffinch, greenfinch and yellowhammer must always have existed in the forests but were probably not nearly as abundant as they are today when they can feed on stubble fields, in stackyards and on the seeds of weeds that are common now but which were rare or absent in forests. Birds of open country such as corn bunting, linnet, skylark, lapwing and many others must also have increased greatly.

Of course it is not only bird populations that have been changed by the loss of our forests. Most other creatures, and plant life too, have been greatly affected. It is interesting to work out which plants and animals may have got scarcer and which may have become commoner with the change from a natural to a man-made countryside.

It might be useful to consider woodlands the other way round and look at what happens if cultivated land is allowed to go back to the wild. Let us imagine a fenced-in ploughed field that is left for nature to play with. What happens? Seeds from nearby hedges and woodlands are carried to the field by the wind or by birds and animals, and it soon gets covered with weeds some small, some tall. Of these the small ones are quickly crowded out by the tall kinds and what is left is a jungle of thistles, docks, nettles and willow herb. But among them will be many seedlings of trees. These have a hard time at first, having to struggle for survival among all those powerful weeds, and some of them die. But others win through and in two or three years are taller than the thistles. After that they develop more quickly, all competing with each other to get the light that is vital to their growth. Meanwhile below ground their roots are competing for the food they seek from the earth.

In the course of time the field will have turned into a thicket of closely growing trees of various kinds such as hazel, birch, ash, beech, oak and sycamore. And because of the shade their leaves cast in summer many of the original weeds will have died away through lack of light. Perhaps after twenty years the tallest trees in the thicket will be the birches because they are a quickly growing species. But in another twenty years, when the thicket has become a real wood, the birches will be far less noticeable for the others will be overtaking them and beginning to crowd them out. Give the wood a further twenty years and great changes will be seen. Trees may look calm enough standing so quietly in the forest. But in fact they never cease from struggling against each other until they have all the elbow-room they require. So gradually the weakest trees get shaded out and disappear leaving the tallest and longest-living to go on and make mature forest. If the ground is a rich moist loam it is pretty certain that of all the trees that originally sprouted in the field, it is the oaks that will eventually do best for this is the soil that most suits them. So although some specimens of other trees will also survive, what the field ultimately becomes is an oakwood. On its way to becoming an oakwood it will gradually have become populated by many plants, mammals, birds and insects that are at home in oakwoods but which were rare or absent in the original field.

The changes which the field goes through on its way to becoming an oakwood are called 'the natural succession'; and the final stage, the oakwood itself, is 'the climax'. Once a wood has reached this climax stage then it will remain much as it is for a very long time to come. So, if left undisturbed, our oakwood could go on being an oakwood for many thousands of years provided that the climate goes on producing the same average temperatures, wind and rainfall. The only change that seems possible is that gradually the soil conditions might alter and eventually become unsuitable for the growing of oaks. For soil has a life of its own and even in the apparently steady conditions of an oak forest it may gradually change and become more suitable to other sorts of trees. If that happened these other trees would gradually take the place of the oaks. But we really know very little about such soil changes because they proceed very slowly indeed.

What I have been saying about a field turning into an oakwood is not just guesswork. It has actually been seen to happen. Last century such a field was allowed to go back to the wild: a hundred years later it had become in fact an oakwood. So if for some reason everybody left the British Isles, taking their farm animals with them, then in a hundred years most of the lowlands would be covered by oak forest. In chalk districts of south England there would probably be beech forests because oak does not flourish on chalk and beech does. In wet places (which would have greatly increased because no drainage would have been done) there would be swamp vegetation surrounded by alders and willows. High mountain regions would still be open grasslands but their lower slopes would be covered by mixed forests of birch, mountain ash, Scots pine and other conifers which have been introduced to Britain from foreign countries.

A word about these conifers. We have seen how for many centuries the farmers of Britain (and the Continent) have taken over the most fertile land for agriculture, leaving the woodlands to make do on less fertile ground. This means that anyone who wants to create a new forest to-day will almost certainly have to plant it on poor or very poor land. This will most likely be on mountains and moorlands, or sand-dunes or even bogland if it can be sufficiently drained. In such places oak, ash, beech and other deciduous trees make poor, very slow growth but several kinds of conifer do better. So this century, when for reasons of finance Britain has tried to reduce her huge imports of foreign timber by developing new forests, the favoured trees have been conifers, mostly spruces. Since the 1920s exotic conifers have been planted in many parts of the British Isles and more plantations are still being made. The result is that there is in Britain to-day a fair-sized area of conifer forest which, though quite unnatural, is important in its effect on wildlife and so is of great interest to the naturalist.

CHAPTER 2

OAKWOODS

IF man had never come on the scene, clearing away vast numbers of trees over the past two or three thousand years, there would be, south of about latitude 60°, an almost continuous belt of mainly deciduous forest stretching right across the Continent and into Britain. The mountain ranges, poking up above the tree-line, and certain marshes and lakes would be almost the only areas quite devoid of woodlands. In this deciduous forest by far the commonest tree would be the oak, for of all trees the oak is best adapted to survive in the climate and most wide-spread soils of the region. Many other deciduous trees thrive in lesser numbers in Europe's forests but generally only the beech comes near to rivalling the oak, especially in central Europe. Along its northern edge the deciduous forest includes a lot of birch; along the south there is much Spanish chestnut. In the latitudes where the oak thrives best the winters may be decidedly cold (down to $-5°$ C in January) with periods of snow and frost. There is often plenty of summer rain, and the total annual fall of rain (or snow) though varying widely from place to place is not usually much below 508 mm. (20 inches) a year.

Oak is a very successful genus of trees throughout the temperate world, so much so that it has branched out into over 450 distinctive species. Of this large number only twenty-seven are native in Europe and of these only two are vastly abundant: the pedunculate oak and the sessile oak: these are the two oaks which are native to Britain.

Man has introduced other oaks to Britain, mainly as ornamental trees, and to a slight extent some have become naturalised but none of them is numerically important. Among these introduced species are the holm oak or ilex, an evergreen from the Mediterranean region; the Turkey oak, a deciduous tree from south-east Europe; the cork oak, an evergreen from south-west Europe; the Lucombe oak, which is a hybrid between the Turkey and cork oaks and so has evergreen tendencies, some individuals keeping their leaves until the end of the year and some throughout the winter. There are also a few introduced American oaks: these, especially the red oak, have been especially used by the Forestry Commission to provide much-needed colour along the edges of sombre spruce plantations. The leaves of the red oak are a delightful yellow in spring, green in summer and go magnificently scarlet before they drop in autumn.

As for our two native oaks, it must be admitted that the differences between them are not at all obvious: in fact only foresters and botanists ever bother to distinguish them. Yet though they are superficially alike there are real differences between them which we must be able to recognise if we are going to look at our oakwoods intelligently. So let us examine them.

The pedunculate oak is sometimes called the common oak but this is a poor name for a species which in some districts is the less common of the two. Another name occasionally used, the English oak, is also misleading, for there are several parts of England where this is not the dominant oak. So the name 'pedunculate', though rather a mouthful, really is the best for this oak because it picks out one of its most distinguishing features – the fact that its acorns are mounted on little stalks called peduncles, whereas the acorns of the other native British oak sit directly on the main twigs. For this reason this other oak is called the sessile oak, 'sessile' coming from a Latin word that means 'seated'. Note also the different acorn sizes and shapes: that of the pedunculate oak is usually larger and more elongated; that of the sessile oak is usually smaller and rounder.

But maybe when you look at an oak you cannot find any acorns or they are out of reach? Don't despair: the leaves will help you where the acorns fail. The leaf of the pedunculate oak has little or no stalk, and the base of the leaf turns under in a characteristic little curl called an auricle. The leaf of the sessile oak is quite distinct: it is mounted on a

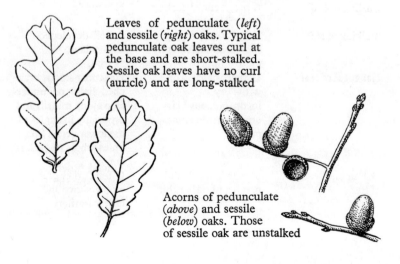

Leaves of pedunculate (*left*) and sessile (*right*) oaks. Typical pedunculate oak leaves curl at the base and are short-stalked. Sessile oak leaves have no curl (auricle) and are long-stalked

Acorns of pedunculate (*above*) and sessile (*below*) oaks. Those of sessile oak are unstalked

definite stalk and the base of the leaf does not curl round to form an auricle. 'Auricle', by the way, means 'a little ear' – a reference to the way our ears also curl at the edges.

If you look at the backs of oak leaves under a lens you will find another important difference between our two native species. Both are hairless on the upper surface and the pedunculate's leaf, especially when mature, is hairless on the underside too. But the sessile oak leaf's underside has branched hairs along both sides of the base of the midrib and larger side-veins.

For quick reference I summarise these differences and a few others in the list below:

	Pedunculate Oak	Sessile Oak
Acorn-cup	Mounted on a stalk (i.e. peduncle)	Growing on main twig
Acorn	Usually larger and longer in proportion than sessile	Usually smaller and rounder than pedunculate
Acorn (colour when fresh)	Light brown with green stripes from top to bottom	Dark brown and not striped
General leaf-shape	Usually broadest about the middle and rounded towards the base	Usually broadest above middle then tapering to base
Lobing of leaf	Lobes are deep and often irregular	Lobes are shallow and regular
Curling of leaf	A pronounced curling or auricle at base	No auricle
Stalking of leaf	Usually only a very short leaf-stalk (rarely up to 7 mm.)	A well-developed leaf-stalk up to 25 mm.
Hairiness of leaf	Usually hairless or with very inconspicuous hairs on underside along midrib	Has conspicuous branched hairs on underside along midrib and especially in angles of the lower veins. Sometimes whole underleaf downy
Colour and texture of leaf	Most often pale dull green and rather thin	Often darker green, glossy above and rather leathery

Buds at ends of twigs	Small and blunt	Large and pointed
Bark	Thick and deeply creviced	Thinner and with shallower crevices
Shape of tree	Trunk is soon lost in crown	Trunk usually persists higher into the crown

NOTE: In examining leaves it is important to get typical ones from as high up the tree as possible and not those growing on low shoots or in shade because they do not run true to form. Also it must be remembered that both oaks, especially the pedunculate, are very variable. Finally it is known that the two oaks interbreed and that therefore hybrids showing characters of both species occur.

The first questions we ought to ask about an oakwood (or any other sort of wood) are: what sort of place is it growing in? Is it wet or dry? Sheltered or exposed? Level or sloping? Highland or lowland? Is the soil deep or shallow? Light or heavy? Fertile or infertile? It is when we have answered some of these questions that we begin to see why oaks flourish better in certain places than in others. We also see that the differences between the pedunculate and sessile oaks are not mere matters of how acorns sit on twigs and so on but that they really are species each with its distinct preferences about where it likes to live and in what sort of soils.

The study of where any plant or animal lives is called 'ecology'. The place it lives in is called its 'habitat'. So now let us look at the ecology and typical habitats of our two British oaks. The first thing to note is that although both our oaks are common trees they are far from being equally common everywhere. On the contrary, in any district where oaks flourish at all, though it is likely that you can find both species, it is also probable that one will be quite a lot commoner than the other. So there is something to do straight away: look at lots of acorns and leaves and decide which is the more abundant oak of your district. Probably it will be the pedunculate oak because this is the commonest and most widespread species. But if you live in Devon, Cornwall, Wales, the Lake District, the Pennines, the Isle of Man, West Scotland or Ireland your oaks may be mostly of the sessile kind. In fact we find so many purely sessile oakwoods in those districts which form what geographers call Highland Britain (see map p. 24) that we might at first assume that the sessile is the oak of Highland Britain and that the pedunculate is the oak of Lowland Britain. But the picture is not so simple as that for the sessile oak is also locally common in the north

Highland Britain. Geographers divide Britain into highland and lowland zones. The highland zone is mainly a region of the oldest rocks; and its characteristic native woodlands, such as survive, are of birch, Scots pine, sessile oak and, very sparingly, ash

Midlands, parts of south-east England and in the New Forest region. And there are fragmentary woods of pedunculate oak on the edges of Dartmoor in Devon, for example, Wistman's Wood near Two Bridges.

Now what about the soils in which our oakwoods are growing? And note that I say oakwoods not just oak trees. For although there may be lots of individual oaks scattered about a district these may not tell us very much about oak ecology. For they may well be growing where they are because someone deliberately planted them there. But an oakwood, especially an ancient oak forest, is more likely to be descended from oaks that have grown on that site for thousands of years, though we can never be sure.

There are three words which need to be understood on our way to grasping the essentials of soil ecology. These words are 'acid', 'basic' and 'neutral', for they describe soil conditions to which large numbers of plants and trees are sensitive. An acid soil (what farmers and gardeners often call a sour soil) is a soil that is lacking in lime. A basic soil (also called an alkaline soil) is soil well provided with lime. Between these extremes, a soil only moderately limy, is called a neutral soil. These conditions in soils can be roughly discovered by chemical indicators which change colour according to the degree of acidity, neutrality or alkalinity. There are also many plants whose presence is good evidence of the acidity or alkalinity of the soil they are growing in. For this reason they are often called 'indicator species'. It is very satisfying to be able to spot these indicator species in the woods, especially if you can check your observations later by soil tests in the laboratory. The degree of a soil's alkalinity or acidity is called its pH.

It is when we come to examine the soils of various oakwoods that we begin to see real differences between the requirements of the two species. What we find is that many sessile oakwoods are on steep hillsides (where the drainage of water past their roots is therefore rapid) and that these hillsides usually have shallow, light, acid and rather low-fertility soils. In contrast, the pedunculate oak is typical of deeper, heavier, basic, fertile soils, the sort of soils you find along valley bottoms, on the clays of London, the Weald or around Oxford, and on the type of stiff clay called gault which lies in a narrow belt around the Weald in Kent, Sussex and Hampshire.

Putting this geologically, we can say that the sessile oak thrives typically on the shallow soils of Highland Britain that have resulted from the weathering of the most ancient (or Palaeozoic) rocks. These rocks may be sedimentary (such as shales, sandstones, mudstones), igneous (such as granites, rhyolites, dolerites) or metamorphic (such as slate). In contrast, pedunculate oak is more characteristic of the deeper soils of Lowland Britain which have come from the less ancient sedimentary rocks. These are what geologists call the Mesozoic and Cainozoic rocks made of sediments deposited in the last 170 million years.

Trees and plants in particular need of lime are called calcicoles: put them into an acid soil and they would die. But some trees and plants love acidity and cannot live in the presence of lime: these we call calcifuges. As for our two species of oak although, as we have seen, one is commoner on acid while the other is commoner on basic soils, these preferences are not so strong that we could use such terms as calcicole or calcifuge to describe our oaks. For if you planted pedunculate oaks on, say, a sour-soiled Welsh hillside they would probably grow quite well, though maybe not as well as the sessile oaks round about. And certainly if you planted sessile oaks in some rich basic soil in, say, the Thames valley, they would flourish far better than they would on a Welsh hillside. In other words it looks as if the sessile oak grows more commonly in the acid soils of Highland Britain not because it prefers them but because most of the richer soils of Lowland Britain have been so successfully invaded by the pedunculate oak that the sessile oak cannot get a real footing in them except in just a few districts.

In this there may be a significant hint about the history of our oakwoods. We can only guess at which of the two oaks first spread across north Europe and into Britain after the last ice sheets melted.

But no matter which came first, it is fairly certain that as each extended its range, there was keen rivalry between them for several thousand years until the pedunculate oak had managed to elbow the sessile oak out of the most fertile regions of Lowland Britain. The pedunculate oak was not, however, adaptable enough to invade the acid soils of Highland Britain except in a very few places, and there the sessile oak has triumphed.

This picture of the British Isles partitioned by the two oak species, with the sessile dominant mainly in the west and the pedunculate in the east, would undoubtedly have been easier to demonstrate in the Middle Ages than it is now. For in more recent centuries a great and largely unrecorded amount of oak planting has been carried out, mainly of pedunculate oak. So now it is difficult to unravel the influence of man from that of climate and soil on the distribution of the two species. Pedunculate oak has been planted more than sessile oak because its timber was believed to be superior (though in fact there is no difference in quality between the two) and because its more zigzagged branches better suited the requirements of the builders of wooden ships. Also the fact that the pedunculate's acorns, and therefore its seedlings, are bigger, has prejudiced man in its favour. They are shed earlier too which is another reason why foresters tended to collect more of them. So in our day the pedunculate oak is probably more widespread than it ever was in the past, whole woods of it having been planted where sessile oaks once grew. So man and nature have worked together to make the pedunculate much commoner than the sessile oak in Britain as a whole.

Let us now consider acorns. And let us go back in time to those oak forests of prehistory which covered so much of Britain, millions and millions of oaks growing as nature arranged them, their trunks well spaced, their branches meeting to form a continuous canopy of summer foliage with an almost uninterrupted spread of shade beneath. What a multitude of acorns these oaks must have produced! Not every year, however, for acorn production is irregular. But now and again there is a phenomenal crop. In such bumper years a fantastic number of acorns must have dropped to the forest floors of prehistory (50,000 acorns per tree is not unusual). But what good were they to the forest, all these myriads of acorns? After all, since in a wild oak forest each tree can be expected to last anything from two to four hundred years (some much longer) there is a need of only a very slow rate of replacement. So countless millions of acorns can disappear and never be missed. And even those which manage to germinate only produce seedlings that soon fail in the shadows of the forest, for oaklets need plenty of light to make successful growth. This means that it is only on the rare occasions when a gap appears in the forest because an old tree has died that there is enough light to encourage a few infant oaks to develop. These will then compete with each other for the privilege of replacing the veteran that has gone.

When an acorn is ripe it drops out of its cup (which may fall immediately after the acorn or may stay on the tree for several more weeks). The acorn is hard and usually weighs about $3\frac{1}{2}$ gm. (pedunculate oak) or $2\frac{1}{2}$ gm. (sessile oak); too heavy to be carried by the wind it falls to the ground below. If there are obstacles in the way, the acorn fall can be noisy, as you will know if you have ever lived in a house overhung by oaks and heard the autumn cannonade of acorns on the roof day and night for a couple of weeks. Or if you go badger-watching in an oakwood on a calm October night you will find, listening in the dark stillness, that the hollow *klink-klonk* of acorns hitting branches as they fall can be really startling.

Nobody seems at all sure what causes a bumper acorn year but it is certainly unusual (though not unknown) for a good acorn crop to be followed next year by another, evidently because the trees are exhausted and need to rest. But think about what happens in a good year. The acorns begin to form as soon as flowering is over in mid or late May. They develop from June to September, growing especially big in a long, warm summer. Then in October the bulk of the acorns fall and under a large, vigorous oak they may lie on the ground below as thickly as a hundred (on average) per square metre. (Sessile oaks with particularly small acorns may produce several hundred to the square metre.)

Then what happens? Of this multitude of acorns perhaps up to a quarter will already have been damaged by insects. (Not that this damage is necessarily fatal: for the woody parts of an acorn can be almost entirely eaten away and yet the acorn may still germinate provided its vital parts have not been attacked.) Few of the acorns, damaged or undamaged, are left to lie on the ground. They are immediately sought by hordes of birds and animals which find them good to eat. Woodpigeons, jays, rooks and pheasants eat enormous numbers by day and mallard sometimes come into the woods and gorge on them by night. Of these birds woodpigeons are the greatest acorn consumers: in fact in the British Isles they probably eat far more acorns than any other creature. They crowd into the woods in October, each bird eating, it is reckoned, about 140 a day (a woodpigeon's crop can hold up to 70 acorns at a time). Not all acorns picked up by birds are destroyed. Jays and rooks for instance, take some away and store them for future use by burying them. Inevitably some of these buried acorns are never recovered and may grow up into oaks. Jays have been recorded burying acorns nearly a mile away from the woods where they picked them up. So we can reasonably assume that jays played a vital part in the original advance of the post-glacial oak forests.

Some mammals also love acorns. Grey squirrels devour large numbers; so do deer, fieldmice, bank voles and short-tailed voles. On the Continent wild boars, and in the British Isles, domesticated pigs (what few are still free ranging) also compete for the acorn crop. Man himself does not normally eat the acorns of pedunculate or sessile oaks because they contain quantities of a bitter substance called tannin which makes them unpalatable and slightly poisonous. Even so they were sometimes eaten in times of famine in the Middle Ages and may well have been important in the diet of early man. Acorns have also been roasted like coffee beans and made into a drink, and sprouted acorns have been used to produce an alcoholic liquor: but both these beverages were presumably rather revolting for they never became popular.

Before we leave the subject of acorns let us go back to the question: what good are they, all these multitudes of acorns that never grow into oaks? Do not assume that they are a complete loss. Those that rot in the ground fertilise it directly. The rest, by becoming food for a host of animals, from microscopic to large, are re-absorbed into the life of the woodland soil and so play an important part in the nourishment of the forest.

Jay burying acorn. In this way jays may have helped in the advance of oak forest after the Great Ice Age

Hobby, a rare little falcon of south Britain, breeding in belts of trees, especially pines, or in open deciduous woodlands

Although long centuries have gone by since the days of the medieval hunting forests there are still remains of them in many districts, the largest being the New Forest which occupies a hundred square miles of Hampshire. Traditionally it is an oak forest: it has both pedunculate and sessile oaks in good numbers with plenty of fine beeches as well as many splendid old yews, hollies and other trees. This century has added a considerable area of Forestry Commission conifers but Scots pine had already been planted there from the eighteenth century onwards and had freely naturalised itself. Wide areas in the New Forest, presumably ancient clearings, are occupied by heathland, grassland and bogs. They are important habitats for a varied fauna and flora. Ponies roam in many parts of the forest and there are roe and fallow deer with a few red and sika deer. It is a heavenly place for entomologists. The list of beetles, for instance, is a record for an area of Britain of this size. Butterfly enthusiasts find the purple emperor there along with lots of lovely fritillaries and some day they may even re-discover a great rarity, the black-veined white, which used to be found there. Rare moths include speckled footman, festoon, triangle and both light and dark crimson underwings. Britain's only cicada (*Cicadetta montana*) is confined to the New Forest area but is seldom seen. This forest is also a place for the very local wood cricket (*Nemobius sylvestris*). Wildflowers practically exclusive to the New Forest are the wild gladiolus and a creeping aquatic plant called Hampshire purslane (*Ludwigia palustris*), a cousin of the willow herbs. The many interesting woodland birds include buzzards, hobbies, sparrow hawks, kestrels and hawfinches; and on the heaths are Dartford warblers, stonechats, woodlarks and stone curlews. An alien bird that has escaped into the forest from the nearby estate of Exbury is Lady Amherst's pheasant which is now quite numerous; but though gorgeously plumaged it is not all that easy to observe for it keeps to the thicker cover. Large flying insects are a feature of the New Forest (hence the insectivorous hobbies and eleven species of bats including the rare Bechstein's): twenty-five of Britain's forty-three species of dragonflies have been recorded in and around this forest which is a principal locality for two of our smallest and rarest kinds, the southern coenagrion and the scarce ischnura. The large marsh grasshopper is another notable insect of the New Forest. The heaths have smooth snakes, sand lizards and the silver-studded blue butterfly; and there is even one locality for tree frogs, an introduction found nowhere else in Britain. Habitats of rare animal and plant species in the New Forest are carefully protected by the Nature Conservancy in consultation with the Forestry Commission and others.

Lying across rolling country between the Severn and the Wye in Gloucestershire is the ancient Forest of Dean which, after the New Forest, is our largest surviving stretch of medieval forest. Its principal trees are also oak and beech, some of the latter having the grotesque shapes of pollards like those at Burnham Beeches and in parts of the New Forest. Besides retaining a few gnarled old veterans both Dean and New Forest have numerous young oaks, both planted and self-sown. A miraculously surviving oak forest of four thousand acres (with also beech, ash, hornbeam and other trees) is Epping Forest in Essex. This very popular forest stretches finger-shaped into London from the north and consists of the remains of old royal hunting forests called Waltham and Hainault. The Field Studies Council has a conservation centre at High Beach where the forest was opened to the public by Queen Victoria on 6th May, 1882. There is a small herd of dark-brown fallow deer and the most distinguished bird is the hawfinch.

Sherwood Forest in Nottinghamshire was made famous by the medieval ballads sung about the outlaw Robin Hood who is now generally accepted to be legendary. Formerly of vast extent the forest stretched west into Derbyshire and north to include the great estates called the Dukeries. Although some ancient woods of oak survive, mainly on sandy soils of low fertility, most of the old forest area is now either agricultural land, brackeny heaths or Forestry Commission conifers. Great oak beams used in rebuilding St Paul's cathedral in the late seventeenth century came from Sherwood Forest. Two or three famous venerable oaks of huge girth survive as tourist attractions. In Sherwood, lepidopterists find the angle-striped sallow as well as other rare moths.

Scattered elsewhere through Britain are the remains of other ancient oak forests. Some of them are still sizeable patches of woodland such as the Wyre Forest in Worcestershire, Windsor Forest in Berkshire, Savernake Forest in Wiltshire, Richmond Park in Surrey and others. The Weald in Sussex, Kent, southern Surrey and easternmost Hampshire was once a great forest called Andredsweald. ('Weald' is an old English word for woodland.) Many forests survive mainly as traditional memories and in place names. Such a one is the Forest of Arden in Warwickshire, the scene of Shakespeare's *As You Like It*. Other former oak forests are now almost wholly Forestry Commission plantations, as at Delamere Forest, Cheshire. Despite all those trees in the New Forest, Hampshire, it is reckoned that Britain's most wooded county is Sussex.

In the early thirteenth century thirty-three counties contained royal hunting forests which were among the most hated official institutions because the laws administering them were terribly severe and restrictive. Though you may not live near any famous old forest it is possible, especially in Lowland Britain, that any small oakwoods you know could be fragments of one of the lesser known forests. So it might well be worth while trying to find out, by a study of place names and local history, whether you can piece your neighbouring woods together to form what was a genuine medieval forest. But if you live in Highland Britain beware of the word 'forest' when it refers to open treeless hunting country, for it probably always did mean that, as it does in Dartmoor Forest, Exmoor Forest, Fforest Fawr (near Brecon) and other moorlands. This use of the word 'forest' goes right back to early medieval times when lands lying outside the fences of estates or parks were all called forests simply because the original Latin word *forestis* (which comes from another Latin word, *foris*) meant 'outside'. So originally forests were 'the outside lands' whether wooded or not. To describe unfenced or 'outside' land that had trees on it, the term was *silva forestis* which meant 'woodland outside (the fences)'. But as time went on the word *silva* gradually dropped out and from then on a forest became popularly accepted as a place of trees. But by then names such as Dartmoor Forest and the names of other open tracts called forests were so firmly established that these places have been called forests ever since though they remain largely treeless.

No doubt the famous oak forests of history grew in favourable conditions. But we should not forget those oakwoods that have survived, however wretchedly, in very unpromising sites. So as you travel round the countryside keep an eye open for these woods that are up against it, battling with gales, high rainfall, thin soils or other miseries. I have mentioned Wistman's Wood of pedunculate oaks high up on Dartmoor. Another wood, typical of many sessile oakwoods of Highland Britain that are afflicted by excessive rainfall, is Coed y Rhygen near Trawsfynydd in north Wales. A wood with a very different problem is Penderi, a reserve of the West Wales Naturalists' Trust. This remarkable little wood grows on the edge of sea cliffs about 10 km. down the coast from Aberystwyth. An evident relic of former forest it is an isolated wood of very stunted sessile oaks clinging to a steep slope above the sea, facing the full strength of the Atlantic winds and frequently blasted with salt spray. It is an interesting wood not only for showing how salt-tolerant the oak is but also because, although the habitat is so unusual, there is just as complete a community of wildflowers in it as you would find in many a wood inland. There is wood sorrel, bluebell, red campion, moschatel, primrose, dog's mercury, pignut, wood anemone, sweet vernal grass and many other typical oakwood plants.

CHAPTER 3

THE UNDERGROWTH OF OAKWOODS

WHEN an ecologist looks at a wood he sees it as consisting of four layers, one above the other like a four-storey building. The plants growing only a few inches high on the floor of the wood are the bottom storey: this is called the 'ground layer' and consists of mosses and other very small plants. The next storey is formed by taller flowering plants and ferns: the 'field layer'. Then above this come bushes and young trees: the 'shrub layer'. Highest of all comes the canopy or umbrella formed by the crowns of mature trees: the 'tree layer'. These four layers are a

The four woodland layers. Each has its special community of animals

PLATE 3. Woods that are National Nature Reserves. *Above*, ancient yews at Kingley Vale, Sussex. *Below*, ash-trees at Rassal in north-west Scotland, Britain's most northerly ashwood.

PLATE 4. Woodland insectivores. Both the common shrew (*above*) and the hedgehog (*below*) are abundant in most types of woodland. Shrews are a frequent prey of owls and other predators, while hedgehogs are much better defended against attack.

useful framework to keep in mind whatever studies you are making in a wood. Whenever you are observing insects, birds or mammals you should note carefully which layer of the wood is their favourite habitat. You might for instance find when watching parties of tits travelling through the woods in winter, that one species feeds mainly in the tree layer while another keeps more to the shrub layer. You then ask yourself why. And answering that question should keep you good for quite a long time. But such tricky problems face the ecologist no matter where he goes.

One discovery we soon make is that not all woodlands have all four layers: the shrub layer, for instance, is often lacking. But most cared-for pedunculate oakwoods on good soil have the complete four layer structure well developed. In some woods mosses clothe almost the entire ground; in others you have to search before you find any. This is simply because most woodland ground mosses flourish in damp and shade. So a wood sloping south will almost certainly have less moss than a north-sloping wood. A wood in west Britain is likely to be richer in mosses than one in east Britain. So woods in river gorges in the west where there is always coolness, shade and moist air are the very best moss habitats. Mosses respond to the chemical nature of the ground just as the flowering plants do. So we have calcicole mosses, calcifuge mosses and mosses that seem indifferent whether the lime-content of the soil is high or low. This means that you will find mosses in pedunculate oakwoods on rich soils which you will not find in sessile oakwoods on poor soils, and vice versa. And you will find other mosses that grow in both types of woods.

Various attempts have been made to give the mosses English names but as they are not, and probably never will be, in general use it is best to use the scientific names only. Among mosses typical of base-rich woodlands may be mentioned: *Thamnium alopecurum, Eurhynchium striatum, Fissidens taxifolius.* In woods on acid soils you are likely to find *Polytrichum* and *Dicranum* mosses along with *Dicranella heteromalla* and *Pleurozium schreberi.* But as your knowledge of mosses increases you will find many more than these in all sorts of habitats, for in the British Isles there are over 600 species.

There is no mistaking the oakwood that is growing on a deep, fertile loam because of the wealth in it of those wildflowers that are indicators of rich woodland soils. There will probably be an abundance of dog's mercury covering large patches to the exclusion of all other species. And where the mercury does not dominate there may be a varied

W.   C assortment of such species as bugle, primrose, yellow archangel, sweet woodruff, wood sanicle, wood spotted orchis, early purple orchis, wood anemone, enchanter's nightshade, wild strawberry, ground ivy, red campion, herb Robert and slender false-brome grass (*Brachypodium sylvaticum*). Permanently wet spots in such base-rich woodland are likely to be occupied by colonies of ramsons, a highly gregarious white-flowered plant that belongs to the onion family and smells like it. Nearly all the oaks in such woodland are likely to be pedunculate. In the district where Cambridgeshire meets Suffolk and Essex, a characteristic

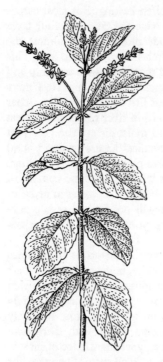

The wood anemone flowers before the tree leaves shade the woods

Dog's mercury, an early spring wildflower common in woods with rich soils

Ramsons, a wild onion that forms large patches in wet woods with rich soils

Wood sorrel often carpets the ground in woods on poor thin soils. Also grows on tree trunks and logs

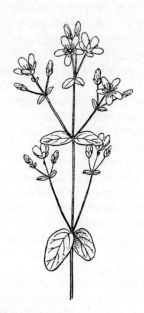

Upright St John's wort (*Hypericum pulchrum*) is commonest in woods with acid soils

Woodsage, common in dry woods and on hedge banks

plant in woods on lime-rich boulder-clay is the oxlip, such a close relative of the primrose that the two often hybridise when they grow near each other. It is feared that the oxlip is gradually decreasing and being replaced by the primrose.

In contrast the field layer of a sessile oakwood on an acid soil is inevitably less rich in species. It is true you may find some of those characteristic of base-rich woods – red campion, herb Robert and wood anemone for instance – but they will probably not be abundant or growing with luxuriant vigour. You are more likely to find some areas deep in bracken, others covered with bramble and others dominated by sheets of bluebells which are the especial glory of such woods. Wood sorrel is another plant which does extremely well in acid woods on thin soils; in fact it demands so little soil it often ramps over rocks and tree stumps and sometimes even grows on the lower boughs of trees, especially in forks. Foxglove, upright St John's wort, cow-wheat, heath bedstraw, tormentil and golden rod are also typical of woods on acid soils. Ferns also do well in such habitats if there is plenty of shade: male fern, lady fern, broad buckler-fern and hard fern being the largest and commonest species. In wetter places you may find the narrow buckler-fern.

A cautionary note: we always need to keep in mind that the soil of a wood, or any other habitat, is unlikely to be of the same quality throughout. More probably it varies from place to place in depth, minerals, dampness, heaviness and other factors. So in a base-rich wood you may find an area of acid sandy ground and get, perhaps, a nice patch of bluebells; or in a predominantly acid wood you may find pockets of better soil that will have sanicle, sweet woodruff or yellow archangel. Still more confusing, you may even find a wood which is such a jigsaw of basic and acid soils that you will find calcicoles and calcifuges growing inextricably amongst each other. A plant grows where it grows not for one reason but many. This means that even in a habitat that does not satisfy quite all of its requirements it can exist, though elsewhere it could flourish more abundantly. For instance, rose-bay willow-herb, which is a light-loving plant, can live for years in dense woodland without ever flowering; but let the trees above it be felled so that it receives the full light of day and it will soon spread and fill a whole clearing with its showy pink flowers. Remember too that some woodland plants are not good indicators because they will grow in such a variety of soils. A good example is wood sage. Provided the shade is only light, wood sage will grow in woods on limestone just as happily as it grows on acid soils.

A wood's field layer is influenced by several other factors such as wetness, steepness and grazing. Here and there you will come upon an oakwood, especially a pedunculate oakwood, with its feet in wet, heavy clay. The field layer then may be dominated by meadow-sweet, stinging nettle, creeping buttercup, tufted hair-grass (*Deschampsia caespitosa*) and various large rushes and sedges. If a wood is on a steep slope you will often find that the plants which apparently demand the most minerals grow down at the bottom of the wood for it is there that the minerals accumulate after being washed out of the slopes above. So you might find a sessile oakwood with little but bilberry on the upper parts of the slope but with such plants as sanicle, water avens and sweet woodruff down at the bottom. For the same reason a gully running down the wood may also be a habitat for such 'demanding' species. Then there is grazing. Many lowland oakwoods are fenced against domestic animals and are beautifully complete in all four layers: ground, field, shrub and tree. But other woods are far less perfect: grazed in by cattle, sheep, horses or, rarely these days, even pigs and goats, these maltreated woods may have their three lower layers reduced to fragments. Particularly in hill districts, the sessile oakwoods form an integral part of sheep-farming, the sheep regularly using the woods for shelter in hard weather for there is no fence between wood and open hillside. The effects of such long-term grazing are unmistakable: grasses are almost alone in being able to survive the incessant attack of close-cutting, incisor teeth, and with no natural regeneration of trees taking place, these declining woods are virtually pastures hardly different from the surrounding grasslands.

A question we can ask about any woodland plant is, what advantage does it get from living in a wood? And what, if any, are the snags? The most obvious advantage is the shelter provided by the trees. Which brings us to the question of climate. Woodlands have a climate of their own. They are shady and cool in summer when the leaves are on; and even when they are bare in winter they still offer a considerable amount of shelter from drying cold winds and are less frosted than neighbouring open ground. Besides, their leaf litter helps to shelter low-growing plants. But perhaps on the whole the summer advantages are most important: excessive heat and drought, two of plant life's worst enemies, are unknown in the shade of a well-developed oakwood.

But though all woodland plants enjoy the dampness, the shade is

another matter. Most, though not all, like plenty of light, so the loss of
light in summer woodlands is the price a plant there must pay for
being sheltered. Oakwood plants have found two ways round the shade
problem. Either they have become shade-tolerant like many mosses
and liverworts and the few plants which flower at full summer, cow-
wheat and enchanter's nightshade, for example. Or they have their
flowers and fruits early in the year, especially in April, just when
maximum sunlight falls into the woods before the leaves of May bring
the shadows. This is a favourite solution and has been adopted most
strikingly by wood anemone and lesser celandine which flower in
March and April. But look for them in July and you will probably find
no sign of them at all, for in June their leaves die down and disappear.
Primroses do not go quite so far as this; they get their flowering over
just as early but their leaves persist through summer. The bluebell
flowers a little later – in May before the shadows get really dense –
but then its leaves die and rot very quickly making the woodland floor
quite slippery for a week or two. So this is something to decide about
any woodland plant we find: how does it face up to the problem of life
in the shadows? Each plant has other difficulties too. How does it try to
ensure the survival of its descendants? How does it spread its seed?
(Wood sorrel seed, for instance, is shot out of the plant a tiny distance by
the explosion of its seed pod but willow-herb seeds float for miles on
the wind). What plants spread by underground runners? Bracken, rose-
bay willow-herb, enchanter's nightshade are among those which do.
Then if a plant flowers in March how can it fertilise its flowers if the
weather is too cold for insects to be flying? One solution to this problem
has been hit on by the violet: some of its buds never form petals and
never open. They fertilise themselves inside the buds (the process is
called cleistogamy) and good seed is produced.

Because most flowering plants need bright light, it is in clearings
or round woodland edges or along rides that you will find many wild
flowers at their best. This means that when a clearing is made in a wood
there is quite a rush to occupy it and this is well worth studying,
especially if you can do it over several years and see the many changes
that are bound to take place – a good example of natural succession.
Certainly, it will be quite different in base-rich woods from that in base-
deficient woods. And sometimes the changes are dramatically swift; I
have mentioned how rose-bay willow-herb can suddenly fill a whole
clearing but other plants such as foxglove can do likewise.

A final aspect of the field layer is a problem the plants cannot do much about. I mean the many caterpillars which eat them. There are even a few kinds of caterpillar which feed on oak leaves at first then descend on their silken threads to eat the plants of the field layer. One is the chestnut moth, common in woods throughout the British Isles.

Several butterfly caterpillars feed in the field layer of oakwoods, notably those of the elegant fritillaries – silver-washed, high brown, pearl-bordered and small pearl-bordered – all on violet leaves. Where

The silver-washed fritillary flies in July and August in southern Britain in woods with violets for its caterpillar to feed on

tufted vetch and birdsfoot trefoil grow in clearings or along woodland edges, especially in south-west England, eastern Gwent and parts of Ireland, you may find the wood white, a delicate-looking, weak-flighted butterfly whose larvae feed on these and other plants of the pea family. A far better known butterfly (though not in most of Scotland or in north and east England), the speckled wood, feeds as a caterpillar on various woodland grasses. In the southern parts of England and Wales (but not Ireland) you may find the comma, a butterfly of the vanessid family (which includes peacock, red admiral, the two tortoiseshells, etc.). It is not entirely a woodlander but is more so than other vanessids and its larvae may be found in the field layer of woods on stinging nettles.

Between the field layer and the tree tops grows the shrub layer. In some oak woods this may consist almost entirely of one species, usually hazel; but in others the shrubs may be varied. Let us look at some of the shrub species one by one.

Hazel has always been the commonest undershrub of oak woodland. In fact pollen analysis has shown that there was such an enormous abundance of hazel in parts of the Boreal Period that it is possible that the land was covered almost entirely with hazel forests before the oaks

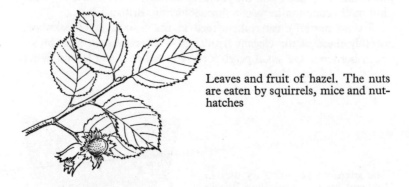

Leaves and fruit of hazel. The nuts are eaten by squirrels, mice and nut-hatches

got established. And still to-day the hazel remains one of the most vigorous, irrepressible shrubs we have. From man's point of view it is a shrub of outstanding virtues: it is pliant and tough and therefore has many uses; it lives long, grows quickly and no matter how often you cut it down it springs up again; for this reason and because it resists the wind it makes a first-class hedge; what's more it bears early pollen for hive bees and edible nuts in autumn.

It is the perfect tree for coppicing. This word, from the French *couper*, to cut, was introduced by the Normans in the eleventh century and from then until early in the twentieth century the coppicing of hazel remained a most important rural occupation, especially in the Midlands and southern England. Hazel stems had an enormous number of uses in the countryside and a considerable acreage of them was cut annually on a systematic rotation. Each section of hazel coppice was cut every so many years ranging from seven to fifteen according to the locality (in damp, very fertile woods hazel grows twice as quickly as in dry, less fertile woods). So in a seven-year coppice a man or a team of men would be responsible for an area of coppice that would take seven years (cutting in winter only) to cut over completely: by which time the first section had grown up again and was once more ready for cutting. The former chief use of hazel was for making hurdles which were joined together in long lengths to form the temporary fences that were much in demand before the Enclosure Movement, for in those days there were very few hedges and permanent fences. Wattle fencing, very skilfully made, is still used for sheep folds, and as wind-breaks round gardens. Other uses for hazel include pea and bean sticks and rustic poles; but many uses – as hoops for barrels, firewood, house-building (walls of wattle and daub) and so on – belong chiefly to the past. The hazel coppices (or copses) are therefore going rapidly out of use: in fact most have already been converted to more profitable forms of forestry.

In the past hazel has often been planted (for coppicing) on really fertile ground because it was a truly valuable crop. But oak too was always in such demand that in many hazel coppices oaks were also planted. Of course they were not cut when the hazel was coppiced but were allowed to grow into full-sized or 'standard' trees, as they were called. This system of growing hazel with oak is therefore known as 'coppice with standards'. Many lowland oakwoods, cut into squares by rides, are still clearly recognisable as coppice with standards even though neglected and no longer coppiced.

Because hazel has been so widespread and abundant for so long in the British Isles it is to be expected that many insects have learnt to feed on its leaves, some no doubt having been introduced to hazel by being blown by the wind off the leaves of higher trees. Besides various small moths (Microlepidoptera), the larvae of thirty or more larger moths (Macrolepidoptera) have been recorded as eating hazel leaves. Among the hazel eaters are two of the great oak-defoliators: winter moth and mottled umber. The list also includes lobster moth, coxcomb prominent, buff tip, pale tussock, lackey, green silver-lines, large emerald and clouded magpie. None of the larger moths is exclusive to hazel and only one is named after it: the nut-tree tussock.

A green shieldbug 13 mm. long (*Palomena prasina*) is sometimes very common on hazel leaves in southern Britain. Another abundant hazel insect, named the delicate apple capsid bug (*Malacocoris chlorizons*) is 6 mm. long and feeds on mites as well as sucking hazel leaf sap. A nut-weevil (*Circulio nucum*), related to the weevils which attack acorns, passes the larval stage eating the inside of hazel nuts from which it

The nut weevil (7 mm.), is abundant on hazels in summer. Its larvae feed on the nuts

emerges when the nut is on the ground in autumn. It then pupates in the soil and the beetle emerges the following spring.

Hawthorn is well known as a hedging plant and certainly it grows strongest and flowers and fruits best in the open. But it is not un-common in the shrub layer of oakwoods though there it grows with less vigour and produces far fewer berries. Possibly its main original habitat was in glades and around woodland edges. But hawthorn is far better known as a hedgerow tree and I shall have more to say about it in Chapter 14.

Holly, in natural oakwoods, is a common shrub or small tree for it grows on almost any type of soil and tolerates shade easily, though in such places it flowers and fruits very sparingly. If it flowers it does so in May, the month in which it also sheds some of its leaves, replacing them by new pale-green ones. Each holly is either a male or a female tree which is why only some hollies – the females – have berries. (Plants and trees with this arrangement are called dioecious whereas most other kinds of trees have male and female flowers on the same tree and are called monoecious.)

A noteworthy insect of this tree is the holly blue butterfly (except in Scotland and most of the north of England). Its life cycle is fascinating. In spring this lovely lilac-blue butterfly with black-spotted, paler undersides, lays her eggs on holly flower buds. The well camouflaged caterpillars (they look like yellow-green woodlice) then eat the flower buds and later the unripe berries. They pupate in early summer and become butterflies in late summer. But these late-summer butterflies, unable to find holly buds at that time of year, lay their eggs on ivy instead. So the autumn caterpillars eat ivy buds and berries before passing the winter as pupae fastened to ivy leaves by silken threads. The holly blue often flies higher than most blues and is the blue butterfly most likely in gardens. In the northern part of its range, in-cluding Northern Ireland, there is a spring brood only. And even in the south of England two broods are unlikely if the summer is cool and wet.

Blackthorn is hardly important inside oak woodland but can be prominent in clearings or margins where it gets more light. One of its peculiarities is that shoots may spring up from its roots several feet from the main stem and if these suckers, as they are called, are not cut back or eaten by cattle they will multiply and spread out into the pasture and form a thicket which may be impenetrable because so armed with thorns. Such blackthorn thickets are great spots for birds' nests, especially woodpigeons, magpies, blackbirds, thrushes and, in parts of Britain, turtle doves. Many moth caterpillars live on blackthorn and so do two distinguished butterflies. The brown hairstreak, a September butterfly, attaches its eggs to blackthorn (often in the angle where a thorn grows out of a twig); there they remain all winter unless picked off by sharp-eyed tits. This little butterfly is probably not as uncommon as most naturalists think: it is just that it does not fly very much, spends most of its time hiding in the blackthorn thickets and rarely visits flowers. It is found mainly in the southern parts of England and Wales. The other blackthorn butterfly is also a hairstreak but it is a great rarity: the black hairstreak. In the counties of Huntingdon, Northampton or west Buckingham you may have the luck to see it about midsummer. Its eggs, like those of the brown hairstreak, pass the winter glued to the bare twigs.

Many other trees and shrubs have in the course of time managed to get into the hazel coppices, most of them being found in the shrub layer of natural oak forest. Which species you can expect to find in which oakwood depends largely on whether the soil of the wood is dry or damp, basic or acid, and what part of the British Isles you are in. But some shrubs are almost universal. Bramble, for instance, spreads in many types of oakwood until it covers great areas. It not only spreads by seedlings but has another device: for if a branch arches over and meets soft ground or dead leaves its tip will take root, so forming a point from which new shoots will soon spring. It is a pestilential weed to have in a wood because it makes walking an agony or an impossibility. It does not even offer the compensation of a haul of blackberries in autumn because in shade it has no flowers. Worse still, it suppresses the woodland wildflowers over which it ramps. It has however this virtue: it shelters many a fallen acorn from the birds, many a young tree from sheep and deer. Perhaps you think all these masses of prickly brambles may provide excellent nesting places for warblers, hedge sparrows and other birds. In fact this is not so. Most birds are not very attracted by large unbroken stretches of dense woodland. A better place for small birds is a wood where the shrubs are well scattered and varied so that the birds have plenty of room to fly about and a wide choice of food supplies. The best habitat of all is the woodland edge.

So when a wood with a dense shrub layer is taken over as a nature reserve the best way to improve it is to make clearings in the shrub layer so as to provide inside the wood as much habitat as possible that resembles a woodland edge.

Other species, some widespread, some local, of the shrub layer of oakwoods include raspberry, wild rose, honeysuckle, ivy, dogwood and guelder rose. All have their special place in the community and have their own insect populations.

In addition to all the shrubs that may be found in an oakwood, we have to remember that there are likely to be young specimens of forest trees such as oak, ash (often very abundant in the shrub layer), sycamore, beech, wych elm, birch, mountain ash, holly, alder, willow, crab apple, field maple, yew and wild cherry. Many of these, provided they grew tall and straight, have always been cut and used as coppice wood along with hazel. Then there is rhododendron. This is a foreign shrub from south Europe which has been planted mainly to provide pheasant cover in those woods on acid soils which normally lack a shrub layer. It was also planted along woodland paths to shelter people from the winter winds. It grows well in acid sand and in peat and though fairly slow growing, it will spread in course of time until it completely fills a wood, killing all smaller species with its dense evergreen shade. Some woodlands, of oak, pine or other species, become completely impassable because of rhododendron. Getting rid of such a jungle is a great problem for the forester who has to rehabilitate a neglected wood. Rhododendron is not only tiresome to clear because of its intertwining branches, it is also useless because its boughs are never straight. Worse still, new shoots spring up very readily from the stumps. Grazing and browsing animals do not eat rhododendron and extremely few insects live on it. But it has one virtue to save it from total disgrace in the eyes of naturalists: flocks of small birds find welcome shelter among its thick leaves on cold winter nights and sometimes quite a few woodcock lie by day on the ground beneath.

No natural woodland, however much dominated by one species, ever consists entirely of that species. So in an oakwood there is at least a scattering of other trees. What they are depends, as with the shrub layer, on where the wood is and on the nature of its soil. In the British Isles there is no native forest tree that cannot be found in some oak-

wood somewhere, so many having been planted there by man.
Some of them, especially ash and beech, grow very well in oakwoods,
having won a place there without the aid of man. But conditions have
to be especially favourable to them before they can begin to dominate,
as I will describe in other chapters.

CHAPTER 4

INSECT LIFE IN OAKWOODS

BECAUSE oak forest is the natural cover of so much of Europe, because oak leaves and acorns are nutritious and because oak leaf-fall produces such very fertile ground under the trees, it is inevitable that the number of species of oakwood animals exceeds that of any other sort of woodland or indeed of any other land habitat. Many of these animals are microscopic, the bacteria for instance which inhabit the leaf mould in vast multitudes. But there are large numbers of tiny but easily visible animals which you can find in any oakwood in summer without much trouble: in fact of insects alone there are several hundred species.

By searching the leaf litter you will find earthworms, springtails, mites, thrips, ants, woodlice, centipedes, millipedes, beetles in all

A springtail, one of a group of very small, extremely common insects that help the decomposition of leaf litter. (Much magnified)

The flat-back millipede (20 mm. lives in leaf-mould

stages, moth pupae and lots of other small animals. You may not put a name to many of them but at least you will appreciate what a host of creatures are always hard at it helping to break down the chemicals in raw animal and vegetable matter and so cause a quicker release of nourishment into the soil than would otherwise be achieved. Finally they all enrich the humus with their bodies when they die. Aiding the animals in the breaking-down process are the fungi, some large but many microscopic. Some (the mycorrhiza) live intimately with oak roots, enabling them to extract minerals from the soil. Others are enemies, attacking the oak in all its parts including the acorns you find blackened and dead. Most toadstools of oakwoods are also found in other broad-leaved woods. Among brackets, the beefsteak injures living oaks; the daedalus grows on dead wood including even buildings.

Insects can be the most impressive inhabitants of oakwoods when they are in sufficient multitudes to strip off all the leaves. Among the eaters of oak leaves, the caterpillars of three moths deserve special mention as defoliators on the grand scale: the oak tortrix (also called the green oak-roller), the winter moth and the mottled umber. When in late spring you see oaks laid bare by caterpillars, you can be certain that there is a plague of one or other of these moths, or maybe all three.

The oak tortrix is the best known because it is on the wing in summer and when super-abundant can be shaken out of the oak boughs in clouds. It is a small nocturnal moth, usually of an attractively brighter green than the dark-green leaves of July. But some specimens are so pale-green as to be almost white. Its caterpillars are also small and green, and being tasty to birds they protect themselves as well as they can by rolling up a leaf by the aid of silken threads and using the resultant cylinder as a den. In times of plague this sheltered sort of existence gets more difficult to achieve as the leaves are shredded and life becomes a battle for the last remaining food. But in a normal year the caterpillar and then the chrysalis live comfortably wrapped up inside the rolled leaf.

The winter moth is larger (2 cm. wing-span) than the oak tortrix. It is one of those drab, greyish little moths which we see often enough (for it is very common in gardens, orchards and woods in autumn and early winter), but rarely take notice of. But fruit growers, even if they cannot recognise the moth, know its effects well enough for its attacks on fruit trees are just as severe as its attacks on oaks. Its female has only tiny wings and is flightless; when she hatches from the chrysalis in the ground at the foot of the tree she climbs the trunk to meet the male moths and often lays her eggs high up in the branches. It is to stop her progress up the tree that some fruit growers fix sticky bands round the trunk a few feet above ground.

The mottled umber is about one and a half times the size of the

Male (*left*) and wingless female mottled umber whose larvae are among the oak's chief defoliators. Look for the moth in autumn or early winter

winter moth and is far less dingy. The forewings vary greatly from white to deep brown and there is often a jagged dark band across them. You may find several varieties inhabiting the same stretch of woodland. The females are wingless, emerging from their pupae in the leaf mould any time in autumn and winter. Like those of the winter moth, these females need to be sought for at night when they crawl up the trunks of oaks and other trees. Close searching with a torch will often reveal a few, but those most easily spotted are the ones that have been found by a male, for the two when coupled together are obvious enough. Incidentally if you have never examined tree trunks on winter nights you will be surprised at the number of creatures to be found on them, especially on mild wet nights. Besides moths you may see woodlice, centipedes, slugs, snails, beetles, spiders; there is also a species of red earthworm which commonly climbs several feet up trees after dark, especially those with mossy trunks. But even on frosty nights you will find the winter and mottled umber moths as active as ever.

The caterpillars of these three major oak defoliators hatch just before the leaves appear so that they are waiting in hungry millions ready to attack the foliage as soon as the buds begin to open. Though so tiny they exist in such myriads in plague years that each leaf is reduced to a skeleton as quickly as it develops. If, however, there is a cold spell in May and the opening of the buds is delayed, then the waiting caterpillars die of starvation and the oaks that year have a good season. But if the worst happens and the trees are seriously defoliated the trees will make little growth that year. So when an oak is felled and its annual rings examined, the years of caterpillar plagues are detectable by the poor growth the tree then made. Not that the health of the trees seems affected for they are adapted to these onslaughts. Besides, the worst caterpillar attacks are quickly over, and in late June or July the oaks often get a second partial clothing of leaves called the Lammas growth (Lammas being an old name for harvest festival when it used to be held on the first of August).

You can see from the time-table below how the caterpillars hatch in early spring and so are poised ready to attack the leaves right from the start. In response to this great caterpillar harvest the maximum number of small woodland birds, tits, flycatchers, tree creeper, nuthatch, starling, chaffinch, etc., are feeding their young just when the caterpillars are commonest.

PLATE 5. Small woodland rodents. Bank voles (*above left*) can be very common especially round woodland edges. Woodmice (or long-tailed fieldmice, *below*) are very numerous in nearly all woodlands. The dormouse (*right*) is found mainly in southern Britain but is believed to be declining in numbers.

PLATE 6. As the grey squirrel (*left*), introduced from America, has spread over much of southern Britain this century, the squirrel (*below*) has declined. The grey thrives best in hardwoods but red seems better adapted to survive in conifers.

Birds and the life cycles of the oak's main defoliators

	JANUARY	FEBRUARY	MARCH	APRIL	MAY	JUNE	JULY	AUGUST	SEPTEMBER	OCTOBER	NOVEMBER	DECEMBER
Oak tortrix (*Tortrix viridana*)	o	o	o	o	l	lpi	i	o	o	o	o	o
Mottled umber (*Erannis defoliaria*)	i	io	l	l	l	l	p	p	p	pi	i	i
Winter moth (*Operophtera brumata*)	io	o	o	l	l	p	p	p	p	i	i	i
Maximum number of small birds feeding young (B)					B	B						

o=ova (egg)   l=larva (caterpillar)
p=pupa (chrysalis)   i=imago (adult moth)

Not that the birds – though each pair takes thousands of caterpillars –
can have a noticeable effect on a population of insects running into
countless millions in a single oakwood. It is only in years when caterpillars are below average numbers that predation by birds may be
significant. It is the oakwoods of the southern half of Britain which
chiefly suffer from these caterpillar plagues. Farther north and west
defoliation is normally less severe for two reasons. The first is that
these moths, like so many insects, flourish more in the milder climate
of the south. The second, perhaps more important reason, is that they
evidently find sessile oak leaves less to their taste than those of the
pedunculate oak; it is noticeable that even in the south of England a
sessile oak is often less attacked than neighbouring pedunculate oaks.

There is a tendency for these defoliators to attack the crowns of trees
first. In this habit there is probably considerable survival value because
all these three species have caterpillars which are quick to drop off the
leaves if a twig is shaken by birds or by the wind. When this happens
they do not fall to earth but hang suspended from silken threads

which their bodies produce through a tiny hole in the lower lip. If the threads are short (as normally those of the oak tortrix are) then the larvae can climb quickly back up them; but they can be several metres long (as in the mottled umber) in which event the caterpillars either rely on the wind drifting them to some low bough or they simply remain suspended for a long time before making any attempt to climb back up again. So the higher up the tree they begin their descent from, the better are their chances of catching on to branches lower down. For once they reach the ground their hopes of ever finding a tree and getting back up to the leaf zone are very poor.

Sometimes fruit growers who have been careful to put bands of sticky grease round their trees to stop the progress of the wingless winter moths are dismayed to find their trees attacked all the same. This is easily possible because a winged male, when paired with a wingless female, may sometimes happen to air-lift her over the sticky band. Also, in windy weather if there are non-protected trees round about, the caterpillars, when tiny, can be swung many metres on to the protected trees as they hang on their long threads of silk. By no means all the caterpillars you see dangling from threads have been knocked off the leaves. When full-grown they use the threads as rope-ladders to convey them safely down to pupate in the leaf mould.

It is not only birds which prey upon the caterpillar multitudes: there are also various flies such as the many species of four-winged flies (Hymenoptera) of the three groups called braconids, ichneumons and chalcids. Most lay their eggs near, on or into the body of a cater-pillar so that their own larvae can live as parasites within its body, ultimately causing its death by slow degrees. In addition, some of the two-winged flies (Diptera) also attack caterpillars, one of the com-monest in woodlands being a bluebottle-sized black fly called *Zenillia vulgaris* which lays its eggs on a wide range of caterpillars. We may assume that this vast array of predatory flies are, in most years, an important control on the numbers of moths in an oakwood.

There are also beetles which prey on the caterpillars, notably a beetle called *Calosoma inquisitor*. The family to which it belongs, the ground beetles (Carabidae), are typically carnivorous but this one is remarkable in being a ground beetle which has taken to a tree life and climbs up high oaks in search of caterpillars especially those of the oak tortrix and winter moths.

There is even a moth caterpillar which joins in the attack on the oak's defoliators: this is the larva of the dun-bar moth, a locally common

Calosoma inquisitor, a predatory
beetle, crawls about oak leaves
eating caterpillars

Dun-bar moth larva which eats
oak leaves and sometimes other
caterpillars

species which can live on leaves or caterpillars whichever are available. Entomologists are therefore careful to isolate the white-striped,
green dun-bar caterpillars from other larvae in their rearing cages.

Besides the three plague-producing moths I have described, there
are many other species whose caterpillars feed on oak leaves (as well as
on other trees). To mention a few: there is the oak beauty, a fine, large
moth that flies in spring and often comes to lighted windows near oak-

Oak beauty, a fine moth of March
and April

woods; the scarce umber (despite its name sometimes common in the
woods of England and Wales but rare in Scotland and Ireland); the
copper underwing (locally common in south England); the common
and the small quakers (found almost throughout Britain); and the
green and the scarce silver lines (two moths notable for their lovely
green colours). The caterpillar of the blotched emerald is remarkable
for its camouflage; it covers itself with oak bud scales which it
attaches with silk to the bristles on its body. Other moths whose
larvae can live on oak include: vapourer, merveille du jour, brindled
green, satellite, flounced chestnut, March, maiden's blush, red-
green carpet, autumn-green carpet, November, light emerald,
canary-shouldered thorn, scalloped hazel, scalloped oak, swallow-
tailed, early, spring usher, dotted border, pale brindled beauty,
peppered, engrailed, leopard, green long-horn and others. About
130 species of larger moths (macrolepidoptera) have been found

eating oak. In addition there are many species of smaller moths (microlepidoptera) which do so. (The oak tortrix moth belongs to the microlepidoptera.)

Not all oak caterpillars eat the oak itself. Instead a few of them live on the lichens that clothe the bark and some manage to resemble those lichens very closely. Because lichens are evergreens, some of the caterpillars feed on them all through winter. About seven species of footmen moths feed as larvae on tree-bark lichens; so do the dotted carpet moth and the Brussels lace. Most of these moths are commonest on, but not restricted to, oaks for the lichens grow on other trees as well.

It is a surprising fact that out of Britain's sixty-six or so species of butterflies only one of them feeds, as a caterpillar, on so universal a tree as the oak. It is the purple hairstreak, a small species that is on the wing in July and is usually common wherever there are oakwoods in most of England and Wales but is only local in Scotland and Ireland. Its habits are unusual: it does not wander about visiting flowers as many butterflies do but remains confined to the oaks, often high up and probably sucking at a sweet substance called 'honey-dew' which greenflies deposit on the leaves. So this is not a butterfly we are likely to see unless we look carefully. (Most of the purple hairstreaks I see are noticed by chance when looking through binoculars at birds.) On a sunny day these dark little butterflies (the females have the brightest flash of purple) can be seen fluttering among the oak leaves. This hairstreak spends most of its life as an egg (August to March) and its caterpillar is yet another of those which are ready to eat the leaves as soon as they uncurl.

Though only one butterfly caterpillar feeds on oak leaves there are several species which you can expect to find on the wing in mature oakwoods, especially where there is a good variety of undergrowth and wildflowers, and where there are plenty of glades to let in the sunshine here and there. Nearly all are commoner in the south of Britain than the north, some being quite absent from Scotland and Ireland. Commonest actually within the woods is the speckled wood which flies in the dappled sunshine of woodland rides in spring, summer and autumn. I have mentioned this and several other butterflies in connection with the field layer (page 39). Outside oakwoods more than in them because it is a sun-lover, you will find the gatekeeper or hedge brown (July and August). Much less widespread (in fact some are very local) are purple emperor, white admiral, heath fritillary, chequered skipper and Duke of Burgundy. The purple emperor, one of the largest and loveliest of our butterflies, is also one of the most elusive

Purple emperor, a very local
oakwood butterfly of southern
Britain

because its delight is to feed on the highest oak leaves (presumably on honey-dew). But occasionally it flies among the oak tops, or soars high above them, tantalisingly out of the reach of anyone who would like a close interview with this fine insect. But though characteristic of oakwoods, as a caterpillar it feeds on willow leaves. It is found only in woods of the southern half of England and in Monmouthshire. Sometimes it may be attracted to the ground by baiting for it with carrion, say a decaying rabbit placed in a sunny clearing in the forest. Like the purple hairstreak, the purple emperor does not normally visit flowers.

The white admiral (no relation of the red admiral and, in fact, a fritillary) is much more approachable for it feeds at bramble blossoms in clearings in July and August and is found fairly commonly in the larger woods of southern England. Its caterpillar feeds on honeysuckle leaves and spends the winter wrapped in a leaf girdled round by silken threads and fastened to a twig. The white admiral has much increased this century. Not so another southerner, the heath fritillary, which remains a very local woodland butterfly from Kent to Cornwall though its food plant, the cow-wheat, is found right to the north of Scotland. The chequered skipper (small, orange-spotted and darkbrown) is even more local, being found in a few mixed deciduous woodlands of the east and south Midlands and in birchwoods in western Inverness-shire, Scotland. These two populations are slightly distinct from each other in appearance which suggests they have long been isolated. They even feed on different species of grass. The caterpillars live from July to March in tubes they make from grass stems and the butterflies are out in late May or June. A similar little butterfly though of quite different family is the Duke of Burgundy which is local but not uncommon in flowery woods mainly of south England in May and June. Its caterpillar eats primrose or cowslip leaves. The Duke of

Burgundy is an insect of special interest, being the only member in all Europe of a large family of butterflies, the Riodinidae, which are found mainly in South America though also represented in Africa and elsewhere.

Butterflies and moths are only one section of the five hundred or more species of insects which make their home in oakwoods. (Of course, many of these insects are not confined to oaks but are also found in other types of woodland.) Some are so small and well hidden you will never see them unless you seek them carefully. I have mentioned those in the leaf litter; there are others that live behind loose bark on trunks; or within rotting hollow trees; others feed quite openly on leaves. Some, the thrips for instance, of which there are scores of species, are minute sap-suckers found on many small flowering plants as well as on trees. They are usually only a few millimetres in length and have two pairs of feathery wings on which they can be floated great distances by the wind. For this reason they are not at all confined to woodlands. Other plant-suckers are the plant bugs or capsids (Miridae): in oakwoods one called *Cyllecoris histrionicus* (4 mm. long) is abundant. Much larger, the shield-bugs, so-called from their flat shield shapes, are also equipped to

Pentatoma rufipes, a shield-bug common in oak and other woodlands. It eats both leaves and caterpillars

pierce and suck leaves: several species may be found on oaks, notably the forest bug (*Pentatoma rufipes*) which, in its immature stage, not only attacks leaves but also caterpillars.

With about 3,700 species of beetles recorded in the British Isles it is inevitable that oakwoods abound with them. I have mentioned (page 50) one which is carnivorous (*Calosoma inquisitor*) and there are others, ladybirds for instance which feed on aphids; but many are vegetarians living on decaying wood, leaves and fungi. In the leaf-litter there may be plenty of rove-beetles (Staphylinidae) but nearly all the many species are minute and known only to specialists. They manage to fold their long wings under very short wing-cases – an astonishing performance. (The devil's coach-horse, which threatens with its jaws and curling tail, is a large and well-known member of this family but it is a beetle of open country rather than woods.) The weevils are another prominent group, often recognisable by their snouts, some of which are long and down-curved. They feed on leaves, flowers, seeds, bark and wood: in fact all parts of trees and plants. Several species, in the larval stage, bore into and eat the heart out of acorns on the trees. When the acorn has fallen they chew their way out and pupate in the soil. In another weevil species the female rolls the tip of an oak leaf into a tube to make a shelter for her young; to make the leaf-tip curl into the desired shape she makes a neat cut right across it, carefully leaving it anchored to the rest of the leaf by the midrib. Eventually the leaf-tip shrivels and falls, taking its occupant with it, but by that time the weevil larva is ready to pupate in the leaf-litter.

A big oak beetle which blunders into rooms at night is the well-known cockchafer or May-bug. It has a red-brown wing case (powdered

Cockchafer, a large, common beetle whose larvae live underground feeding on roots of trees and farm crops. The adults eat leaves, especially oak

white when newly emerged) and a long, pointed, down-curved tail that looks like a sting but is harmless. The males are distinguished by their large, fan-like antennae. The adult cockchafer eats oak and other foliage and in plague years has been known to strip whole trees of their leaves. As well as in woodland, cockchafers flourish in cultivated land and there the large, white, curled larvae can do great damage to the roots of crops in the three or four years of their underground existence. Rooks are great eaters of cockchafers, picking the adults off the oaks in May and digging the larvae out of arable fields near the woods whenever the ground is being ploughed.

A famous oakwood insect is the stag beetle though I am sure its

The greater stag beetle (Europe's largest beetle) is locally common in southern England. Its larva lives in old stumps, usually oak

picture is known to thousands who have never seen the beetle itself. Its popularity rests on the outstanding size and shape of some males – nearly eight cm. in length and equipped with large antler-like jaws which are opened with a great show of menace though in fact they are not nearly as harmful as they look. The female, lacking these over-developed jaws, can bite much harder. Stag beetles are restricted to the southern half of England but even there they are only locally common, as for instance on the outskirts of London. They fly on warm summer nights and occasionally come indoors into lighted rooms; or you can find them by day on tree trunks and fences. The larvae live for several years eating rotten oakwood and may be ten cm. long by the time they pupate. The adults feed by sucking the sweet sap out of oak twigs. In captivity they will eat honey.

A great many other beetles pass their larval stage, often of several years, boring into living or rotting wood or tunnelling under bark where their workings leave beautiful patterns. One important group are the longhorns which live in a wide range of habitats including oak and other woodlands. On old trees, especially oaks, in the southern half of Britain, you may find the largest longhorn of all – the tanner beetle

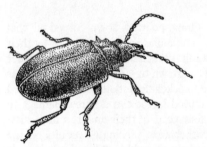

Prionus coriarius, a large longhorn beetle whose larva feeds inside the base of rotting trees

(*Prionus coriarius*), a strange insect sometimes nearly five cm. long with heavy-looking saw-like antennae and a thorax armed with three teeth on each side. Most longhorns are much smaller and more slender but they have the long antennae, especially the males, and their larvae all bore into wood. A particularly beautiful wood-borer is the cardinal beetle (*Pyrochroa serraticornis*) whose larvae live under the bark of rotting oaks and other trees. The beetle itself is magnificently scarlet all over and about two cm. long. It is frequent in southern England but local or absent elsewhere in Britain.

The oak bush-cricket is common mainly in southern Britain. It is active at night among oak leaves but hides by day from birds

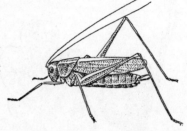

Compared with moths and beetles some groups of insects are poorly represented in our oakwoods. In the grasshopper family, for instance, there is but one common species and even that one is common only in England and Wales, being absent from Scotland and rare in Ireland. It is the oak bush-cricket (*Meconema thalassinum*), the only British grass-hopper or cricket which lives in trees. It is a beautiful insect, a delicate pale-green all over, with very long, slender antennae. It is about in late summer and autumn; and at night it sometimes makes short flights from oaks to settle on lighted windows or come indoors.

Galls are a fascinating subject and there are few better places to see them than in an oakwood. Galls are abnormal growths upon a plant or a

A gall wasp. These remarkable insects go through two generations each year, their summer galls being quite different from their winter galls

tree and serve as a home and a source of food for their occupants. They may be caused by four-winged flies (such as gall-wasps and some saw-flies), two-winged flies (such as gall-midges) and also certain fungi. Just what process causes a gall to form has not yet been fully explained, but it is assumed that some chemical is injected by the insect or fungus into the tissues of the host plant and that this so interferes with the development of hormones (substances which stimulate growth) that the plant's energy is diverted into the production of excrescences which are of no apparent use to the plant, though often of no great harm.

The best known galls on oaks form a particularly varied group; all are the work of gall-wasps and include the following: marble galls, oak apples, artichoke galls, currant galls and spangle galls. Let us look at

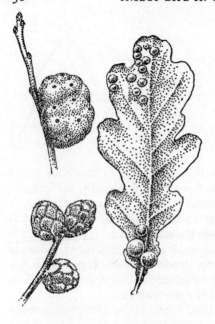

Oak galls: *left upper*, oak apples; *left lower*, artichoke galls; *right upper*, spangle galls; *right lower*, marble galls

them in that order. Marble galls are hard, smooth, marble-sized spheres closely attached to oak twigs and are the result of buds being infected by the gall-wasp *Andricus kollari* when she lays her eggs in them in spring. Though there may be many marble galls on one spray, each contains only one gall-wasp egg. After summer you will find these galls have a neat round hole in them through which the newly-hatched gall-wasp has emerged.

Oak apples are larger than marble galls and are soft, spongy and irregular in shape. Creamy-white at first they eventually become pale-brown with reddish streaks. Unlike the marble galls each oak apple contains a dozen or so wasp larvae which emerge each through its separate exit after midsummer. The females, having mated, descend to the ground and burrow down to the rootlets of the oak and there produce clusters of small, dark-brown, subterranean root galls from which in December or January there emerges a generation of wasps which are all females. These then climb the trees and, though there are no males to mate with, lay fertile eggs on buds at the ends of twigs. The buds then develop in a deformed way, soon wrapping each egg separately in cellular matter and so more oak apples are produced. The gall-wasp responsible is called *Biorhiza pallida*. Understandably for many years oak-apple galls and oak-root galls were thought to be the work of different species of wasp. All these gall-wasps are black and very small (two or three mm. long) and so are not at all like the large, black and yellow insects we normally call wasps.

Artichoke galls are formed on the ends of oak twigs and consist of little clusters of what look like pale-brown scales which give them the appearance of a tiny globe artichoke. Inside these scales is the real gall, very small but hard and nut-like. As with the oak apple there is an alternate generation. This is reared from tiny inconspicuous galls attached to oak catkins. The artichoke gall-wasp is *Andricus fecundatrix*.

Currant galls hang in strings like red currants from the oak's male catkins. Normally these catkins, having shed their pollen, soon wither or fall. But those infected by gall-wasps remain firm enough to support the currant galls. These galls, which also form on leaves, are the alternate generation of the gall-wasp (*Neuroterus quercusbaccarum*) which causes spangle galls.

Spangle galls are reddish little domes 5 mm. across and sometimes numerous on the backs of oak leaves. These galls fall off the leaves in autumn with their larvae inside them, then the leaves fall and hide them. In early spring the gall-wasps emerge and fly up to the oak buds to lay the eggs that will cause the currant galls.

You will find various other galls upon the oaks. Most have alternating generations like the above and some, if you keep them in a jar, will produce other insects besides gall-wasps. For galls are popular habitations for 'lodgers' ('inquilines' is the proper term) – enterprising insects who have learnt to take advantage of the food and shelter offered by the galls.

CHAPTER 5

BIRDS OF OAKWOODS

MANY birds can be found in oakwoods but they differ greatly in how much of their total lives they spend actually in the woods. Some use them merely as seasonal dormitories. For instance the wood I look at from my house provides a roosting place for a large flock of jackdaws during the winter. Every morning at first light they go away to feed in distant fields. Every evening they come home to roost; but they are never there during the day the whole year round. A small party of stock doves which roosts at the other end of the wood does just the same.

In contrast there are the birds which, night and day the whole year round, never leave the woods except for occasional safaris along hedgerows or into gardens and orchards. Tree creeper, nuthatch and great spotted woodpecker are perhaps our best examples of these thoroughgoing woodlanders, but no birds belong to oakwoods alone; most of them frequent all other sorts of deciduous woodland at times.

Once we can identify the birds of a wood – they are all fairly easy, especially in spring when those otherwise difficult warblers help us by their songs – a question we can try to answer is, how does each bird get its food? And you soon see that the different species have found different ways of finding enough to live on. For a highly specialised woodland bird take the tree creeper. It spends a great proportion of its

The tree creeper is specialised for climbing up bark and finding insects in crevices

waking life climbing trees. As it gets near the top of each one, it dives to some point lower down on a neighbouring trunk and climbs up that one, ascending in quick jerks, pressing its stiff-feathered tail against the tree to steady its climb, picking out minute insects from crevices in the bark, for which its thin, curved beak is perfectly adapted. No matter how many flies are in the air near a tree creeper it will ignore them all, except that very occasionally it will lean over backwards and snap one that comes really close. Flies are just not its meat unless it finds them on the bark of trees.

In contrast a spotted flycatcher will spend a long time on one perch, flying out and round every few minutes to collect a fly from the air, snapping it up with a noise you can hear. Another specialist is the great spotted woodpecker. Not interested in flies nor in insects in bark-crevices, this woodpecker's prey is wood-boring grubs – the larvae of

The great spotted woodpecker eats nuts and visits bird tables but is specialised for digging larvae out of dead trees

beetles and moths. To get them it has to cling in one place on the trunk for quite a while and make many hammer blows with its bill. So, like the tree creeper, it has evolved strong sharp claws for clinging. Its tail is strong and hard-feathered so that it can rest on it as if it were a third leg. Its beak is large, tough and sharp for chiselling into the wood, its neck muscles are extremely well developed and its head is protected by a thick-walled skull which acts as a cushion against all the hammering. Unfortunately the woodpecker's most remarkable feature is one we have little hope of observing in the field (though we may possibly be shown it on a film): this is the lightning way its extremely long and flexible tongue whips into holes to pluck out the wood-boring grubs.

Perhaps it may strike you that woodpecking is a hard and slow way of getting a meal. After all, fly-catching would be so much easier. Or why not just dig for worms in the ground like a thrush? But we must not forget the cold of winter. Then there are no flies and the fly-catchers have had to retreat as far as Africa to be sure of a regular supply; and the thrushes may be dying because worms are unreachable in the frozen earth. Meanwhile the great spotted woodpecker carries on just as in summer, working its way methodically through the forest from one dead tree to the next, getting its food by this hard but sure method, whatever the weather. For this reason it is also better adapted to survive than its relative the green woodpecker. At some time in its evolution, the green has tended to neglect the art of woodpecking and has found it easier to go to the fields and peck ants out of the soft earth of ant-hills. But if you are a bird that specialises in ant-eating you pay for it in severe weather when the ant-hills are frozen solid or deep in snow. So in severe winters green woodpeckers often die while great spotted woodpeckers carry on happily, as untroubled by the frost as are the wood-protected grubs on which they feed. Besides, the great spotted can also live on acorns, nuts and pine seeds; and increasingly it takes the splendid variety of titbits offered on bird tables.

There is a further point about the green woodpecker: in taking to ant-eating it has become rather less strictly a woodland bird and more a bird of parkland where trees are scattered among pastures, the sort of habitat where ant-hills are more plentiful than in woods. For it is on the meadow ant, the species that builds the mounds common in some grass-lands, that this colourful woodpecker mostly feeds. You may wonder: what about wood ants – doesn't the green woodpecker eat them also? Yes, it does in districts where the wood ant exists. But the wood ant is a rather local insect and not at all typical of deciduous woods, being commoner among pines whereas the green woodpecker prefers de-ciduous trees.

Our third woodpecker, the scarcer and far more secretive lesser spotted, is strictly a woodland bird with a preference for oaks, though it may be found in any large deciduous timber and also old orchards. It is less a bird of tree trunks than of small outer branches where the bark is thinner to peck through for grubs. It therefore feeds high and, being silent most of the year, it easily escapes notice.

The nuthatch is a real oakwood bird (south Britain only), for two of its chief sources of food are acorns and hazel nuts, which it splits open after carefully wedging them in a crack in a tree. Hence the name: nut-hatch is really short for 'nut-hatchet', and when you see how neatly it

The nuthatch is adapted for running up, down or across trunks and branches in search of insects. It also splits hazel nuts

cleaves a hard hazel nut in half you will agree the name is a good one The nuthatch has specialised on rather woodpeckerish lines and has become a hammerer. But acorns and nuts are only seasonal foods. At other times of year the nuthatch has to behave more like a tree creeper and live on the insects and spiders which shelter in crevices on tree trunks. But whereas the creeper concentrates its attention on the trunks of the trees the nuthatch is less a trunk bird than a branch bird and so avoids direct competition with the creeper for food. Also it is a head-down bird not a head-up bird like a creeper or a woodpecker, and so has not evolved a specialised long, hard tail; its tail is in fact short and soft. But to enable it to be the most acrobatic of all bark-clingers it has large, strong toes and much-curved hind claws so that in its favourite position, which is sideways, it hangs on one leg and supports itself by the other. By climbing across or down the bark, the nuthatch is perhaps able to spot insects which the up-climbing tree creeper is liable to miss.

An oakwood is such a varied habitat offering so many different sources of food, that inevitably it harbours lots of birds that are not nearly as specialised as tree creeper, woodpecker and nuthatch. But because a bird has no very obvious peculiarities we should not conclude that it is not specialised in some less striking way. So whatever woodland bird we see we can ask ourselves what particular qualities this bird has for getting a living among trees.

Of tits we can certainly say that one of their specialisations is their energetic and lively movements which they can keep up all day long in their search for food: in winter this may consist largely of very tiny insects found on twigs and bark, every surface of which is searched by these highly acrobatic birds. Another tit speciality is the short but stout bill which is capable of cracking open nuts.

When we see flocks of mixed tits in the winter woods we should not hastily assume that they are in serious competition for food. It is more likely that by subtle differences in food preferences, methods of searching and level of feeding, the birds are carefully sharing a wider range of prey than the human observer might at first think possible. Blue tits and great tits certainly show a tendency to keep slightly apart when feeding, the blue tit preferring the tree layer while the great tit favours the shrub layer.

Two other woodland members of the tit family, marsh tit and willow tit, are very alike, for both have black caps and grey-brown bodies. The marsh tit is badly named for it is not a marsh bird, but the willow tit is a little more aptly named. For though you may find it in many types of wood, it belongs mostly to thickets round the edges of bogs and swamps, often on sour, acid ground where the trees may be willows, alders, birches or conifer plantations. But the marsh tit tends to favour richer habitats and is more typical of well-grown oak-ash woods.

It must be emphasised that the idea of birds keeping to their special level or storey of the woodland can easily be exaggerated. Diagrams showing such zonation make things look far more neat and orderly than they ever are in nature. For instance though great tits are typical of the shrub layer they often feed in tree tops, and habitually do so in woods without any shrub layer. And in years when the oak tops are really crawling with caterpillars there are very few small birds which do not forage up there when feeding young.

Like the tits, the warblers are beautifully adapted to woodland life without having specialised in any very remarkable degree. With their slender bodies and quicksilver actions they can slip quickly through leaves and closely set twigs and find and pick up caterpillars and spiders in very large numbers when they are feeding their young. But though so specialised to find food on both the tops and undersides of leaves they are not adapted to detecting insects hiding in the bark of trees and so they could not survive our northern winters. True, a tiny number of blackcaps and chiffchaffs occasionally winter in Britain, mainly in the south, but the vast majority of the huge population of warblers which inhabit our deciduous woods in summer are in African woodlands from September to April.

Seven species of warbler – willow warbler, chiffchaff, wood warbler, blackcap, garden warbler, whitethroat and lesser whitethroat – are regular inhabitants of oakwoods. In watching them it is interesting to observe how their feeding places differ from each other so that they compete with each other as little as possible. The chiffchaff tends to feed high up in the tree layer; but its close relative, the willow warbler,

PLATE 7. Woodland owls. The tawny (*right*) is our commonest owl, well known for its beautiful hooting cry. The shorteared (*below*) is a moorland owl but it often breeds among newly planted conifers where voles are plentiful in long grass.

PLATE 8. *Above left,* the tree creeper, an insect eater, finds practically all its food as it climbs up the bark of trees. *Right,* the nuthatch is more adaptable, moving up, down or across with equal ease and eats not only insects but also nuts. *Left,* the green woodpecker nests in trees but is often a ground feeder, living on ants.

The wood warbler nests on the ground in woods where undergrowth is sparse

habitually feeds in the shrub layer. So in those damp oakwoods where willow is dominant in the shrub layer, the name 'willow warbler' suits this bird well enough, but in the drier woods 'hazel warbler' would be a better name. Another close relative, the wood warbler, is more like the chiffchaff in feeding high up. But a difference between wood warbler and chiffchaff is that while the chiffchaff requires some development of shrub layer, such as brambles, in which to nest, the wood warbler prefers woods with few or no shrubs for it builds its nest right on the ground.

Blackcap and garden warbler, closely related to each other and with very similar songs, nests and eggs, can be fairly well distinguished by their habitats. Though both are common in oak and other woods with a thick shrub layer, the blackcap usually feeds and sings higher in the trees, whereas the garden warbler is more skulking, feeds more in the undergrowth and places its nest in more hidden, thicker bushes. These differences are most clear when the two species are nesting in the same wood. But where there are no blackcaps the garden warbler often sings from the tree tops.

The habitats and feeding habits of whitethroat and lesser whitethroat can be similarly distinguished. Both species may breed in the same oakwood but the lesser whitethroat prefers less dense undergrowth and so is commoner along the woodland edge, whereas the whitethroat may inhabit a really thick shrub layer. Also, while the whitethroat often nests low down in brambles, the lesser whitethroat builds higher – five or more feet above ground – a favourite site being a very prickly hanging curtain of wild rose, especially the field rose (*Rosa arvensis*) which has long, slender, blackish twigs.

The place of the nightingale in the woodland jigsaw is an interesting one. All the small birds we have so far looked at are birds of bush or tree. So, too, is the nightingale but with this difference: that for feeding it usually goes down to the woodland floor where it searches the leaf-litter for worms, beetles, ants, ant pupae and other small life. As it not only feeds on the ground but usually does so under thick cover, it would be one of the least known of woodland birds if it were not such a noisy and persistent songster by night as well as by day. The nightingale is not confined to oakwoods; yet though it also breeds in shrubberies, overgrown hedges and wet thickets, there is often even then an oak or two in its territory; and its nest, which is on the ground, is often based on dead oak leaves. Also, though mainly a ground feeder, it has some-times been seen to feed its young on caterpillars off the oaks, especially the little green ones of the oak tortrix moth. The nightingale is rather particular in its choice of habitat: by no means every oakwood is to its liking though it is impossible for us to see why. The preference seems to be for a wood of well spaced deciduous trees, particularly oaks, with dense patches of rose briar, bramble, nettle or umbellifers. Unfortun-ately this intriguing bird is virtually restricted to those parts of Britain south and east of a line from the Wash to the middle Severn and even there it has decreased in recent years.

The robin, so familiar in our gardens and on our bird tables, is a close relative of the nightingale. (Adult robins and adult nightingales may look very different but their mottled brown young are very like each other.) Though it has adapted to many man-made habitats unacceptable to the nightingale, the robin is unquestionably of forest origins. In many parts of the Continent it is still only a shy bird of deep cover, and in the British Isles, as well as being a garden and park species, it remains a common woodland bird. Like the nightingale, it feeds mainly on the woodland floor and probably on similar food. Even so, the two species are not necessarily in direct competition for, while the nightingale feeds under thick cover, the robin forages more in clearings.

Some birds are so unspecialised about their methods of finding food they seem to belong to all levels of the woodland. The redstart, for instance, though generally a low-level bird taking insects and spiders off the ground, is also often in the tree tops, the male especially, where he may sing conspicuously from the highest twigs and often flutter out for flies. Found in many kinds of woods such as oak, birch and pine (but not spruce), the redstart is particularly common in some of the steep sessile oakwoods of the west and north, yet it is curiously rare in Ireland. Like so many birds, it seems to prefer those parts of woods where plenty of sunlight gets in; it is therefore far less typical of denser thickets than are its relatives, the robin and the nightingale.

The redstart nests in holes – in trees, walls or in the ground – or in all sorts of odd places: I once saw a nest in a carpenter's workshop. It was made entirely of wood shavings and placed on a shelf among chisels and saws. As a hole-nester, the redstart finds itself in fierce competition with other hole-nesters such as tits and nuthatches, and the scarcity of suitable holes can seriously limit the number of such birds that can nest in certain woods. You soon realise the importance of holes if you install nest-boxes in a wood where natural holes are rare: there is usually an immediate increase in hole-nesting birds. This can

Redstart (*above*) and pied flycatcher are both hole-nesters breeding locally in British woodlands

be shown most dramatically in those parts of Britain, mainly Wales, the Lake District and the Scottish Border where the pied flycatcher is abundant. No bird takes more readily to boxes and if you put up, say, a hundred boxes in an oakwood in those districts, you may easily get over half of them occupied by pied flycatchers. Of course some of them would have nested in the wood in natural holes, but the boxes undoubtedly cause a great increase in population. Yarner Wood near Bovey Tracey, Devon, never had any pied flycatchers until nest-boxes were provided. The birds occupied the wood immediately, yet there had been no breeding colony so far south in England before then. The mystery in such a colonisation is where all these additional pied flycatchers suddenly come from.

Commonest of all woodland birds, the chaffinch illustrates the choice that faces small insectivorous species: to get through the winter they must either emigrate as warblers and flycatchers do, or learn to find tiny animals on bark and twig as tits and creepers do, or they must drastically change their diet. The chaffinch has assumed this last habit: it feeds on woodland flies and caterpillars in spring and summer; then in autumn and winter it becomes mainly a seed eater foraging in fields by day and only coming to the woods to spend the night. In many a wood in the late afternoon from October to March you can see large numbers of chaffinches arriving in twos and threes and often making swift corkscrew dives to their sleeping places. These mass roosts may be used winter after winter then be suddenly and mysteriously abandoned.

The increasing, thrustful starling has established a niche for itself in woodlands as in many other habitats. Perhaps its first choice for a nesting place is in or near human settlements. Then, having fully occupied such sites, it spreads through the countryside. In woodlands it nests in holes in trees, especially those made in previous years by woodpeckers; but quite often it drives woodpeckers away from nest-holes actually in use. Young starlings are first on the wing just when the oak caterpillars are at their most abundant and for a week or two the tree tops are loud with the churring hunger cries of the birds being fed by their parents. But the caterpillar harvest is quickly over and from then on, except for roosting, the starlings ignore the woods and become foragers in fields.

Oakwoods of the Highland Zone are a characteristic habitat of the buzzard and, in Wales, of the red kite also. But this is not by preference: it is simply that these larger raptors once nested in woodlands all over Britain but have been exterminated by man over large areas of the lowlands. So although the kite in Wales may seem to prefer to nest in steep woods of sessile oak, this is because steep sessile oakwoods are so typical of the part of Wales where the kite has managed to survive.

The smaller, more widespread sparrowhawk is a typical raptor of oak and other broad-leaved woods. But its preference is for mixed woods where it often finds it easiest to place its broad shallow nest on the flat boughs of larches. It likes woods with open country around where it can hunt the small birds of field and hedgerow.

In a wood managed as coppice-with-standards there develops a regular succession of breeding birds as the coppice develops. In the first spring after clearance of the shrub layer, birds are rather few because both nest-sites and food are restricted, but the wide spaces between the big trees are acceptable to tree pipits, yellowhammers and other ground nesters. Then, in a couple of years, the shrubs are growing quickly into bushes and these species disappear, being replaced by warblers, thrushes, hedge sparrows and bullfinches which now find many breeding places. But in another few years the hazels, ash poles, chestnuts and so on are getting tall and tree-like and more suited to hold the nests of woodpigeon, turtle dove and jay, and the numbers of small birds decreases. Then the coppice is cut and the cycle begins again. As for the standard trees, their supreme bird is undeniably the carrion crow, for the crow builds its nest in the oak tops, roosts up there the whole year through and uses them constantly as a lookout when danger threatens. Omnivorous and highly adaptable, the crow feeds to some extent on the woodland floor but more often on open ground outside the woods. Though this bird is called the 'carrion crow', it is probable that carrion is only a minor part of its diet which consists mainly of earthworms, insects and any other small animals it can catch, together with seeds, acorns and other vegetable matter. The crow is not the most popular of birds. Long and thoroughly persecuted it shows amazing resilience and remains abundant. Anyone wanting a woodland bird to study for its success against what seem to be heavy odds in the struggle for existence need look no further than the carrion crow.

CHAPTER 6

WOODLAND MAMMALS

WOODLAND can be rich in mammals – far too rich, a forester may complain, when he sees the damage done to young trees by deer, rabbits, squirrels, mice and voles. But the forester, trying to establish artificial plantations, necessarily takes a narrow view of woodland mammals. In natural forest it is evident that there is a healthy balance between the trees and the mammals since both have survived together for thousands of years.

What mammals you will come upon in a British oakwood will partly depend on what district of Britain you are in. For instance you may well find roe deer in a wood in Scotland, north England or extreme south England but are less likely to do so elsewhere. In a few north Scottish oakwoods, those alongside Loch Maree in Ross and Cromarty, for instance, you might be lucky enough to see a wild cat (though you would stand a better chance in the pinewoods). Oakwoods in Wales and bordering counties are certainly a habitat of polecats. In woods of Sussex and Hampshire you might chance upon a colony of the rare Bechstein's bat in a hollow tree. In woods in parts of Hertfordshire and Buckinghamshire there are colonies of an introduced rodent, the edible dormouse. But apart from these and a few other localised species, the woodland mammals are widely distributed in Britain, though some are missing from Ireland.

Let us take the smallest mammals first for they are extremely important both numerically and because so many of the others depend on them as food. We might call these little ones the eight-cm. group, for that is about the average size, measuring head and body only. They are so vastly numerous that there must be something particularly advantageous about being in this size group. Three are insectivores: pygmy shrew, common shrew, water shrew; six are rodents: bank vole, wood mouse, dormouse, yellow-necked mouse, short-tailed vole and house mouse. Because all of them are predominantly nocturnal, living in runways in the leaf-litter or among thick grass or other vegetation, they are seldom seen. Yet every oakwood with a full complement of undergrowth has some of them in large numbers. Their populations can be studied by regularly putting down lines of live-traps in the woods. The

Common shrew, an abundant very small insectivore of wood-lands and grasslands

pygmy shrew (5 cm. excluding tail) is found throughout the British Isles but is less a species of deep woodland than of woodland edges and similar light cover. The common shrew (7 cm.) is found in a variety of habitats including real forest where it has been found to outnumber the pygmy shrew by 25 to 1. Despite its name the water shrew (8 cm.), beautifully patterned black above and white below, is quite at home in the heart of woodlands a fair way from water. That neither common nor water shrews are found in Ireland is presumably because Ireland was separated from Britain before these shrews spread into south-east England from the Continent; but both are widespread in England, Wales and Scotland. Shrews feed on a wide variety of invertebrate animals. They are difficult to observe and, trapping apart, are most easily detected as skulls in owl pellets.

Of the small rodents the bank vole (10 cm.) and the wood mouse (9 cm.) are those which most abound in oak woodlands; the wood mouse is much the commoner and, because it lives in fields as well, it may be Britain's commonest mammal. The bank vole is less nocturnal, so if you glimpse a reddish 'mouse' scuttling about even in bright sunlight, this will be a bank vole. (Voles differ from mice in being blunter-nosed and shorter-tailed.) The wood mouse (also called long-tailed field-mouse) has the large, prominent eyes of a strictly nocturnal animal; it is larger than a bank vole, has a far longer tail and is much given to leaping, as distinct from the scuttling of voles. In years when it is very abundant the wood mouse may make a whole-scale attack on the nests of small birds, even climbing high to get at them in holes and nest-boxes. The bank vole also can climb trees and may perhaps be equally destructive. Both these little rodents eat quantities of acorns, and one or the other (perhaps both) hides them underground in little piles; but plenty remains to be found out about this acorn-burying and how ex-tensive it is – an interesting subject for the patient investigator. Both bank vole and wood mouse eat large numbers of insects (animal matter forms at least a third of their diet) as well as berries, nuts and seeds. Both litter their feeding places with hazel shells that have holes nibbled in one side. The wood mouse leaves chewed snail shells lying about; and also has the curious habit of using old birds' nests as feeding platforms, leaving them piled up with the skins of hawthorn berries.

The distribution of the dormouse (8 cm.) in Britain is southern and western but it is absent from Ireland and the Isle of Man. It just reaches

Dormouse, a mainly nocturnal, hibernating, woodland mouse of southern Britain, thought to be decreasing

the Scottish border country on the west but is generally rare north of the Midlands. It is unique among our rodents in its habit of hibernating: in autumn it rolls up in a tight ball, wraps its furry tail round its body and goes into a very deep sleep in a nest often among dead leaves; but occasionally it has surprised people by settling down for the winter in cottage bedrooms. During hibernation its body becomes cold to the touch and it seems quite dead. And though it wakens occasionally in mild weather it does not finally come out of hibernation until April. It lives in many sorts of woodland, including oakwoods, provided there is plenty of undergrowth where it can climb about the lower branches and find seeds, fruits and insects. It likes plenty of honeysuckle in its habitat, using strips of its bark to build its summer nests which are in low bushes. So look out for honeysuckle stems which have been freshly stripped by dormice. Though mainly nocturnal the dormouse will come out in the shade of woods during daylight, especially to suck the nectar out of honeysuckle flowers.

Three other small rodents may be mentioned to complete the picture but their numbers in the oakwoods are not usually important. There is the yellow-necked mouse (10 cm.) which is extremely like a wood mouse but is slightly larger and instead of a yellow spot on its white breast (which is the mark of the wood mouse), it has a yellow band right across from one fore-leg to the other. So whenever you find a wood mouse examine it carefully in case it is the much scarcer yellow-necked, a species well worth reporting to the local Naturalists' Trust. It is unknown in Scotland, Ireland and the Isle of Man and has not yet been recorded from every county in England or Wales. Then there is the short-tailed vole (10 cm.) which, though not characteristic of mature woodland, occurs in grassy clearings and around the margins, and so in some woods can be locally abundant. I shall say more about this vole when I talk about conifer plantations. Finally in deciduous woods, of oak or other species, you may meet with occasional colonies of house mice (8 cm.), for not all live in houses, especially in summer.

Farther up the size scale we find insectivores: mole (14 cm. head and body) and hedgehog (22 cm.), both common in oakwoods. In fact the mole can be really abundant without anyone noticing it because its hills, so conspicuous in pastures or on lawns, often have to be searched for in a wood deep in leaf mould and undergrowth. The hedgehog, too, both a hibernator and nocturnal, is also far commoner in woodland than you might at first suppose. But go into an oakwood after dark on a still, warm summer night and listen; if there are hedgehogs present they will probably advertise the fact by the loud crackling they make as they crawl among last year's leaves looking for slugs. Close to, you will even hear the slugs being crunched in the hedgehog's jaws. Shine a torch and the hedgehog will not run away but will probably carry on with its affairs; fully armed against predators, hedgehogs have little fear.

Two large rodents next: the red and grey squirrels; and two rodent-like animals, rabbit and hare which are separated into an order of their own called the Lagomorpha. Presumably as long as there have been woodlands in the British Isles there have been red squirrels in them except for occasional periods when they have died out locally and have been re-introduced. But to-day this squirrel is decidedly on the decline and has been for much of this century. Can it be mere coincidence that during more or less the same period the bigger American grey squirrel, introduced last century, has spread into many areas of Britain? Is the grey squirrel successfully competing with the red for food and living space and steadily ousting it? Does it perhaps carry an infectious disease to which it has considerable resistance itself but to which the red squirrel succumbs? This seems likely. What happens is that ten years or so after the very first grey squirrels appear in a locality the red normally becomes rare or quite dies out. On the other hand there are places where the red squirrel has become rare without any grey infiltration at all. So it is just possible that the red squirrel would have declined anyway. After all, without any grey squirrels being present, the red vanished from most of Scotland in the eighteenth century but was later re-introduced.

The oakwoods of England, especially in the south and the Midlands, have been almost completely abandoned by the red squirrel and in them the grey thrives abundantly. In towns the grey prospers, when tolerated, in large suburban gardens and parks, sometimes retiring in winter to the lofts of houses. Not that squirrels hibernate, but they like to have their winter nests as well protected as possible. Summer nests of the grey squirrel are large untidy collections of twigs and dead leaves set conspicuously in high forks. Though not so beautiful, to most people's eyes, as the red squirrel, the grey is an attractive animal to see in the woods either rippling along the ground, leaping from bough to bough or sitting nibbling an acorn in its paws. Its diet is varied: acorns are most important but it eats many other nuts and seeds; also buds, shoots, bulbs, fungi, bark, insects and birds' eggs. The grey squirrel is probably more adaptable than the red and is more often found away

The grey squirrel is an American species that has this century replaced the native red squirrel in much of Britain's woodlands

from woods. It sometimes occurs on high moorlands and I have twice seen one in the saltmarshes of an estuary half a mile from trees. It is not always entirely grey: when immature it has much red on its sides and cheeks and is then often mistaken for a red squirrel. In mountainous country, as in Wales for instance, the grey squirrel tends to occupy the large woodlands of valley bottoms and leaves the sparser scrub near the heads of the valleys to the red squirrel. But in most places where the red squirrel still survives in good numbers it does so in pinewoods.

The rabbit is not a native animal of Britain. When introduced by the Normans in the eleventh century, rabbits were kept in enclosures and carefully looked after as a valuable source of food in an age when all meat was a luxury. Where there was no soft soil or sand for them to burrow in they were provided with large mounds of earth which still survive here and there, often being marked on maps as 'Pillow Mounds'. In later centuries, as other sorts of meat became cheaper, people became careless about keeping the rabbit within bounds, so it escaped and spread through the whole of the lowland and semi-upland country-side and became a pest of the fields and woods. This was its status until 1953 when the disease called myxomatosis was deliberately introduced to Britain and quickly reduced the rabbit to its present comparatively small numbers in most parts of the country. (Before 1953 the number of rabbits killed annually in Britain approached a hundred million.) Oakwoods, especially those on the deeper soils of the lowlands, were often infested with rabbits especially along banks round the margins; and in such woods any palatable plants, including seedling trees, had no hope of survival against the combined onslaught of voles, wood mice and rabbits. Planted trees can also be severely damaged by rabbits stripping off the lower two or three feet of bark in hard weather. On chalk downs the cessation of grazing by rabbits after 1953 led to a widespread growth of scrub vegetation and changed the ecology of whole areas. Hares, though typical of open country, frequent woodlands also and can be similarly a forester's pest, though in natural forest the barking of young trees by hares and rabbits would be useful in keeping down excessive regeneration.

Although perhaps most people associate bats with caves, old mines and buildings (especially churches), the fact is that most of our dozen or so species have close connections with woodlands, particularly old woods with big hollow trees. In such trees bats often breed in spring and summer, then many of them retire to caves or roofs for hibernation. And even those which never enter hollow trees, presumably feed in or along the edges of woodlands fairly often; and as their food is often moths we can include bats along with all the other predators who take their toll of the multitudes of woodland insects. Bat-study has increased

Bechstein's bat, a rarity that lives in hollow trees. Mostly recorded in south England

in recent years but much remains to be found out about distribution, habitats and movements. If you are energetic enough to make a survey of the woodlands of a district, you would certainly add to our knowledge of bats, if only on a local scale. And you might be lucky enough to meet with some real rarity such as Leisler's or a barbastelle and so make a discovery of much wider interest. You may even find one with an identity ring on it. If so report its number to London Zoo: they will tell you where your bat was ringed.

In British woodlands there are seven species of carnivorous mammal but two of them, pine marten and wild cat, though once widespread have now become so local through persecution that few naturalists have studied them in the field. Another, the polecat, is common only in Wales. The remaining four: fox, badger, stoat and weasel are still generally abundant except on islands. There are not, and apparently never have been, weasels in Ireland.

All these predators have a varied diet. The fox, a member of the dog family (Canidae), eats small rodents, rabbits, birds, insects especially beetles, berries especially bilberries and blackberries, and carrion. In 1960 it was shown that about 1,300 foxes had died through eating birds, mainly pigeons, poisoned by toxic seed dressings. Badger, stoat, weasel and polecat all belong to the weasel family (Mustelidae). Badgers

Left, polecat; *right,* stoat. The polecat is almost confined to Wales but the stoat is widespread in Britain. Both frequent woodlands and live mainly on small mammals

have an even wider diet than foxes, for they not only eat what the fox usually eats but also enjoy grubs dug out of wasps' nests, many acorns and much beech mast, and large numbers of earthworms which come to the surface of the earth at night. Stoats prefer to feed on rabbits if they can but otherwise concentrate mainly on voles and mice, eating birds and birds' eggs, insects and fruit in season. Weasels have a similar diet and so, probably, do polecats but their diet has not yet been thoroughly investigated in the wild. So there is a challenge to someone with time and enthusiasm to tackle a difficult study.

What all these predators have in common is their position at the end of a food chain. At the start of this food chain there is vegetable matter such as stems, leaves, flowers, fruits, seeds, wood, bark and roots. On these feed all the countless numbers of moths and moth larvae, beetles and beetle larvae, bugs, aphids, bacteria, springtails, mites, flies and fly larvae, gall-insects and so on. On these small vegetarian creatures preys a host of carnivorous insects as well as spiders and others. Prey and predators alike are food for the smaller mammals and birds which also eat large quantities of vegetable matter. Then at the end of the line, eating the smaller mammals and birds, come the hawks, owls and carnivorous mammals whose crucial part in the woodland ecology is in helping to control the populations of the small mammals which in reasonable numbers are beneficial to the forest but which can badly upset the environment if, as sometimes happens, they multiply excessively.

Rises and falls in the numbers of small rodents can have most interesting effects on the breeding success of their predators. It has been shown in the Canadian Arctic that the lemming, a vole-like rodent, increases to peak numbers every seven years and that the population of its main predator, the Arctic fox, follows exactly the same pattern. In the British Isles such dramatically regular patterns are not known (though field voles are said to be more numerous than usual every four years), but plagues of voles have produced large numbers of foxes and a dearth of voles has prevented owls from breeding. For instance in Wytham Wood, Oxford, which has long been closely studied by ecologists, it was found that in 1958 the whole of its thirty pairs of tawny owls failed to breed because, in the wood that year, there were hardly any small rodents for them to feed on. The owls kept themselves alive and that was all. They needed far more food to get them into breeding condition. Possibly such rodent shortages also reduce the breeding success of carnivorous mammals though not as drastically as that of owls. For mammals probably turn to other food supplies more easily than owls are able to do.

Though I said there were seven carnivorous mammals in British woodlands I could have added an eighth – the domestic cat, as any gamekeeper knows. Of the millions of domestic cats in Britain it is fortunate that most live in towns and never go near a wood. But cats on the edges of towns, in villages or on farms very often go hunting in nearby woods and many settle down awhile and raise a family there. So quite a population of rather wild-natured cats can develop in a wood, and though they never seem to survive very long, their presence, while it lasts, must have its effect on the numbers of birds, voles and mice and of rival predators. Since there were once wild cats throughout Britain we may wonder why the domestic cat, so often taking to the woods, has never really established itself in the wild. The probable reason is that the domestic cat is mainly descended from a North African species and so is not fitted to survive the rigours of our northern winters without the food and shelter man so lavishly supplies.

For many people the loveliest and most intriguing of all woodland animals are the deer. Certainly to our medieval forebears the idea of a forest without deer would have been unthinkable. But to-day we accept our many deerless woodlands as we accept their many other unnatural features. And even when deer manage to infiltrate into these woods the picture is far from complete. For what is still lacking are three fine predators which in the wilder Continental forests are a very necessary check on deer numbers. Britain once had these powerful raptors: wolf, bear and lynx, but has long since lost all three. So now it is man who is chief controller of deer numbers, rigorously so in plantations where deer would otherwise do much damage to young trees. For instance, some foresters reckon one fallow deer to every twenty-eight hectares (70 acres) or one red deer to every forty-eight hectares (120 acres) is plenty.

Three kinds of wild, native, hoofed animals were common in British oak and other forests in the early Middle Ages: wild boar, roe deer and red deer (though there were apparently never any wild boar in Ireland). Only gradually, as hunting grew less important and agriculture split the forest into ever smaller blocks, did these animals get scarcer. But the last four centuries have struck at them very hard. The wild boar became extinct early in the seventeenth century. The deer, unprotected for hunting, got slaughtered without mercy as agricultural pests and as a source of cheap meat. The result was that they were exterminated from whole regions especially those lacking large woodlands thicketed with dense undergrowth. The red deer, a larger and therefore easier quarry, was exterminated almost everywhere outside Scotland. The roe, smaller and more elusive, survived much better. The woods on rich lowland soils, having a well-developed shrub layer, sheltered their deer better than did the woods of the Highland Zone where the shrub layer was thin. So parts of England kept their roe deer while wilder districts such as Wales lost theirs entirely.

This century the deer situation in English woodlands has improved, while in most of Wales deer are still very scarce. In England, especially in the north, the spread of Forestry Commission conifers has greatly helped roe deer which thrive in the shelter of young plantations. So there are now roe once more in many areas where they had been exterminated. Roe are now in fair or good numbers in northern England in parts of Cumberland, Durham, Lancashire, Northumberland and Westmorland; and in southern England in parts of Devon, Dorset, Hampshire, Surrey, Sussex and Wiltshire. They are very well distributed on the Scottish mainland but are absent from Ireland.

Wild red deer, though found in small numbers in several English counties where they are the descendants of those escaped from deer parks, are only at all plentiful in north-east Devon and north-west Northumberland. They are common in parts of mainland Scotland but not nearly so widespread as roe. Some Scottish islands, notably Jura and Rhum, have many. But in Scotland the red deer is only marginally a woodland animal, for there the destruction of the forests forced it to adapt to a hard life on treeless moorlands where it does not attain such magnificent size and antler development as better fed deer can achieve in parks and woodlands. Probably the limelessness of moorland soils has much to do with this difference. In woodland on good soil the deer get a calcium-rich diet from the varied and nutritive herbs and trees they find there; this greatly enhances their body growth and antler development.

The fallow deer was introduced from south Europe, presumably for hunting, very long ago (it was well established by the time of Domesday 1086). It is thoroughly naturalised in many woodlands of southern England and is scattered elsewhere in many places. Fallow are the most popular species for deer parks; and those escaping have often founded wild populations nearby. Wales, Scotland and Ireland have far fewer fallow than England. This deer's favourite habitat is deciduous or mixed woodland.

Other deer, but of recent introduction, have also escaped from parks and become naturalised in woodlands here and there. Among them the sika, a smaller Japanese relative of the red deer, is widely but thinly scattered in England, Scotland and Ireland. There is a very small, unobtrusive deer called the muntjac (from India and China) which is local but increasing mainly in southern England. The Chinese water-deer is also locally established in Bedfordshire and nearby counties and also in Shropshire.

With deer generally spreading in British woodlands there are ever-increasing opportunities for the fascinating sport of deer-watching, a far more exacting pursuit than bird-watching if the deer are truly wild. For such deer are excessively timid, much given to keeping in thick cover, have sharp sight and hearing and, most important of all, an equally acute sense of smell. So you need to dress soberly, to wear quiet footwear and to perfect the art of the silent, unseen, upwind approach. You also need to rise early if it is summer, or stay out late, for deer feed mainly at dawn and dusk, and you had best go alone. If you get within eighty metres of deer you are doing very well and with binoculars will have marvellous views. If you stand absolutely still a long time and have a slice of luck as well, you may even have feeding deer pass slowly by you at only a few metres' range. For all details of identification and many helpful hints read *A Field Guide to British Deer* published by the Mammal Society of the British Isles.

Above left, red deer; *centre,* sika; *right,* fallow deer.
Below left, water deer; *right,* muntjac. Of these only the red deer is native in Britain

CHAPTER 7

BEECHWOODS

BEECHES are familiar trees nearly all over the British Isles. In a few places they have undoubtedly descended naturally from the beeches of prehistory. But we can be sure that the vast majority have been put where they are by man or are the offspring of such trees. Most obviously planted are the beeches that form avenues, shelter-belts and hedges or have been placed on hill tops to complete a vista. There are also many beechwoods which are just as artificial; and lots of single beeches looking absolutely wild in mixed woodlands have also been carefully set there by man.

But though beech is so widespread it is only in south England and south Wales that there are beechwoods which can be regarded as natural and even they have been much interfered with by man. You will find these beechwoods on the Chiltern Hills in Buckinghamshire and neighbouring counties, and in the Thames valley nearby; in a narrow circle round the Weald in Kent, Surrey, Hampshire and Sussex; and on the Cotswolds in Gloucestershire. There are smaller fragments in South Wales and on both sides of the lower Wye valley

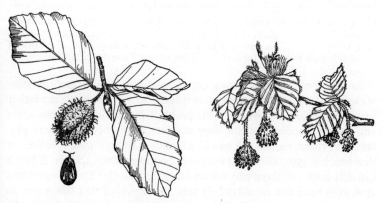

Left, beech leaves and fruit. Beech nuts (mast) are abundant only every few years. They are eaten by many birds and animals. *Right*, beech flowers and young leaves. The female flowers are inconspicuous, the male catkins hang as green tassels

between Monmouth and Chepstow. Some of the old oak forests such as Epping and New Forest also have fine stands of beech which, however, have probably been planted.

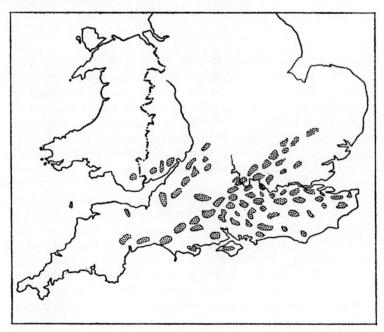

Generalised map of native beechwoods. Beech is widespread in Britain because it has been planted by man. But only the Chilterns, the Cotswolds and a few other places in southern Britain are accepted as the sites of natural beech forest. (Herbert L. Edlin of the Forestry Commission.)

As beech will thrive in almost any soil and its seed will freely germinate as far north as Scotland we may wonder why beechwoods are rather scarce in Britain as a whole. This problem is especially striking when you see the woodland on the deep and fertile soils of the Chiltern plateau. For there, though oak and beech both grow very well, it is evident that beech is quite dominant over oak. So the question then is: if beech can defeat the oak there why not on other fertile soils? This is a problem ecologists have not yet solved. It was once believed that beech was so successful on the Chilterns because it could tolerate the lime-rich soils there. But then it was discovered that although the slopes of the Chilterns have limy soils (being on chalk) the plateau is covered by an acid soil called clay-with-flints. So just what it is about clay-with-flints that favours beech before oak remains to be discovered. It may be a matter of soil texture: lighter soils help the beech, heavier soils the pedunculate oak.

Putting the problem another way we might ask: what is it about the many other soils that evidently favour oak instead of beech? In trying to answer such questions we should not forget the influence of man. It seems that in Britain at any rate man has long rated oak far higher than beech. Oaks produced much more valuable timber. They could also be grown as standard trees amid the very useful coppices whereas beeches are useless as standards because no coppice could grow in their deep shade. So, except in places where it was much used by local craftsmen such as the chair-makers of the Chilterns, beech has probably been persistently weeded out of the forests as something worthless. William Gilpin, writing in 1791, certainly did not think much of beech: 'Its wood is of a soft, springy nature; sappy, and alluring to the worm.' His contemporary, William Cobbett was no more enthusiastic; nor was the woodland expert of a century earlier, John Evelyn, who remarked that beech did not make particularly good timber or fuel. In fact the only quality he admired in the tree was that very comfortable beds could be made by filling mattresses with its long-lasting leaves gathered in the autumn before the frosts. It is possible that in the days of primitive man there were beechwoods that have long since been felled. After all, if men with stone axes wished to clear a forest they would surely tackle beech rather than oak, for many upland beechwoods were probably quite free from undergrowth whereas the oakwoods of the valleys more resembled jungle. Of beechwoods now surviving in Britain, the best cared-for are those on top of the Chilterns for they are used by the furniture industry at High Wycombe. The output of the Chiltern woods is, however, only a drop in the ocean for an industry which gets its material mainly by vast imports from abroad. On the Continent there are still extensive, well maintained beech forests. In Germany, for instance, beech is the commonest broad-leaved timber tree.

Some kinds of trees, like some nations of men, seem ever eager to occupy new ground. Oak, birch and pine for instance. Others are much less thrusting, as if content to hang on to what they hold and leave it at that. Beech is this sort of tree. So although it can thrive on many different soils, alkaline, neutral or acid and so seems fitted to carve out great empires for itself, it does not. The soils on which beechwoods are most successful are: dry, shallow limy soils such as on the Chiltern escarpments, the Weald and the Cotswolds (such soils are called 'rendzinas', a Polish word); deep loams which are mineral-rich but may or may not contain lime – such soils are found on the South Downs and on the

Chiltern plateau; and acid sands such as at Burnham Beeches, Buckinghamshire and Epping Forest, Essex.

A well-grown beech casts a dense shade in summer, it deposits below it a generous bed of leaves, and its roots spread widely, many of them close to the surface. For these reasons a beech makes an awkward neighbour for other trees to live near and for flowering plants and shrubs to grow under. So a typical beechwood on fertile soil is quite free of undergrowth, its floor deeply covered in tawny leaves – beautiful woodland to look at and walk through but of limited attraction for the naturalist. The smothering effect of the leaf carpet lasts many months for beech leaves are very slow to rot down. The few wildflowers that thrive in such difficult conditions either flower in early spring before the beech shade gets too dense or they have special adaptations enabling them to flourish in the gloom. Such specialists are yellow birdsnest and birdsnest orchid. Yellow birdsnest is a curious plant, the sole British representative of a family called the Monotropaceae which is much better known in North America than in Europe. Yellow birdsnest is a plant without chlorophyll, the green colouring matter which is essential to the chemistry of photosynthesis, the process by which most plants take carbon dioxide and water from the air and turn them into carbohydrates and oxygen. Yellow birdsnest survives without photosynthesis by feeding directly on decaying matter such as leaf mould as a fungus does. That is, it is a saprophyte ('eater of putrefaction'). You will find it flowering mainly in July and August when the leaf canopy is at its densest. Nearby you may find the birdsnest orchid which flowers in June or July. It too is a saprophyte and, like the yellow birdsnest, can feed on rotting vegetation because it has allied itself with an underground fungus partner. Both yellow birdsnest and birdsnest

Yellow birdsnest, a very local plant. Lacking chlorophyll it can live in the deep shade of beechwoods

PLATE 9. Oakwood birds. The pied flycatcher (*above left*) breeds mainly in Wales, the Lake District and along the Scottish border. The wood warbler (*right*) prefers woods with tall trees and sparse undergrowth. *Below,* the jay stores acorns in the ground but does not always recover them; those the bird misses may eventually grow into oak trees.

PLATE 10. Birds of Scottish pine-woods. *Above left,* female and young crossbills beg for food from the male. *Right,* the siskin's nest, usually high in a pine, is very difficult to spot. Both crossbills and siskins are often widespread in Britain, especially outside the breeding season, but the crested tit (*left*) seldom wanders far from the pinewoods of the Highlands.

orchid are yellowish or brownish plants not all that easy to see in the deep shade where they grow. The name 'birdsnest' is a reference to their roots which are tangled into a rough ball-shape; but the name is an insult to most real birds' nests which are masterpieces of skill.

The beechwoods with the most poorly developed field layer are those in which the trees themselves are finest – tall, of even age, their thick leafy canopies locking tightly into each other to exclude the summer sunlight. The woods of the Chiltern plateau are of this sort. But where the trees are not so huge and evenly aged and where the canopy is less dense and is broken into by either clearings or light-admitting trees such as ash or oak then the field layer can be quite varied. On steep escarpment woods for instance, where the beeches are varied by whitebeam, wild cherries, yews and hollies, there will usually be dog's mercury, wood sanicle and ivy (carpeting the ground) in abundance. You can also find bugle, sweet woodruff, violets, wild strawberry, yellow archangel, wood anemone, wall lettuce, arum lily, woodspurge; and, more sparingly, columbine, green hellebore, Solomon's seal and spurge-laurel (which is neither a spurge nor a laurel but a daphne). Besides birdsnest orchid, there are three other orchids: common helleborine (which is cross-pollinated by wasps), white helleborine and the much rarer narrow-leaved helleborine.

White helleborine (*Cephalanthera damasonium*) is a lime-loving orchid mainly of beechwoods

Most of these wildflowers are typical of lime-rich soils. But if you go in May to beechwoods on limeless ground you will find a quite different field layer. There you might see sheets of bluebells under the trees or carpets of wood sorrel or brambles. In such woods other trees besides beech are likely to be sycamore, oak or an occasional hornbeam. In beechwoods on thoroughly acid, sandy soils the ground is often patched with bilberry, heather or bracken; and there may be a scattering of upright St John's wort, wood sage, cow-wheat, pill sedge and wavy hair-grass. Two mosses, *Polytrichum formosum* and *Leucobryum glaucum*, are usually abundant. If there is any shrub layer it will be of birch, eared willow, holly and mountain ash. In such infertile ground the beeches themselves are likely to be short and crooked. But the stunted growth of the famous trees at Burnham Beeches is due to pollarding long ago. (Pollarding was the practice of cutting the top off a tree about two metres above ground. This made it produce a crop of small branches out of reach of cattle and deer, thus providing a regular supply of poles and firewood.)

Beechwoods, especially those with a mixture of other trees in them, are well known for their fungi. Come the autumn, and they produce a more splendid profusion of colourful toadstools than you will find in any other type of woodland. Fungi are particularly common in the woods on acid soils covered by a bed of leaf-litter rich in humus on which they

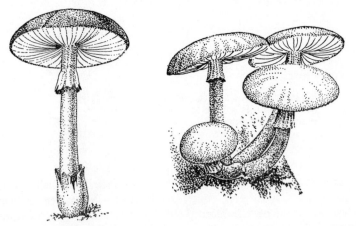

Left, Amanita phalloides (death-cap); *right, Armillaria mucida* (beech tuft). The death-cap, our most poisonous toadstool, is found in deciduous woods especially oak and beech

can feed. Typical toadstools of beechwoods include *Cortinarius elatior*, *Russula fellea*, *Russula lepida*, *Amanita citrina*, *Amanita vaginata* (the grisette) and the very poisonous *Amanita phalloides* (the death-cap) to mention only a few. You can also discover some fine species of fungi, both toadstools and brackets, on the beeches themselves – notably the delicate white *Armillaria mucida* (the beech tuft), *Pholiota adiposa*, *Lentinellus cochleatus*, *Ganoderma applanatum* and *Hericium coralloides*.

Leaf mould in beechwoods makes good hunting ground for those who specialise in small creatures such as springtails, mites, earthworms, etc. Above ground, insect life (especially in a pure beechwood) is very sparse in the shady, plantless conditions under the trees. But up in the canopy quite an assortment of moth caterpillars (but not butterflies) feed upon the leaves. Between forty and fifty caterpillars of larger moths have been found living on beech, some very common like vapourer, winter moth, November and grey dagger; some not nearly so well known such as alder, lobster and scarce merveille du jour. Typical smaller moths of beech include *Chimabache fagella* and *Lithocolletis faginella*. Another enemy of the beech is the felted beech-scale (*Cryptococcus fagi*) which sucks the tree's juices through the bark, dotting it with tiny white woolly tufts which the insect uses to protect itself. There are also the beech aphis (*Phyllaphis fagi*) which sometimes sucks the juices of the leaves in vast multitudes, and a few two-winged flies which make galls on the upper surface of the leaves, and a black weevil (*Rhynchaenus fagi*) which riddles the leaves with holes and mines.

Beechwood moths provide some elegant examples of camouflage: the barred hook-tip and the clay triple-lines are strikingly like the colour of autumn leaves; and a pretty little grey moth called Blomer's rivulet which, though as a caterpillar it feeds on wych elm, usually finds a beech trunk to rest on when it becomes a moth. The smooth beech bark is also welcome to slugs which climb the trunks in wet weather, especially the grey species called *Limax marginatus*.

Of these beechwood insects perhaps none is more remarkable than the lobster moth or, rather, its caterpillar (for the moth looks ordinary enough – large, thick-bodied and dark-brown) when you find one on a tree trunk. The caterpillar, also brown, is grotesque, especially in its threat display: its tail end, which is very thick and swollen, is bent forwards over the back and armed with two bristles. At the same time the caterpillar also rears up the front part of its body and sticks out its extraordinary long thin legs which it vibrates in a menacing manner. What is more, from a gland on its underside, it can send out a jet of

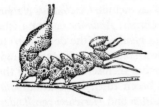

Larva of lobster moth. Widespread but local, this strange caterpillar of beech, oak, birch, etc., squirts formic acid to deter its enemies

formic acid 'certainly powerful enough, if well directed, to disable a small bird' says Dr E. B. Ford in his excellent book *Moths*. The lobster moth is a member of a family called the Notodontidae which includes the prominents, kittens, puss moth and buff tip. Several of them have strangely shaped caterpillars with the ability to squirt formic acid at attackers.

No mammal is peculiar to beech but most of the oakwood mammals, ranging in size from shrews to badgers, are common also in beech-woods. (The beech marten, a member of the weasel family closely resembling the pine marten, was once thought to be British but has long since been shown to be Continental only.) There is one mammal which, without being restricted to beechwoods, is probably commoner in them than in any other sort of wood. This is the fat (or edible) dor-mouse which was introduced from the Continent and released at Tring

Fat or edible dormouse, an alien found in a small area of southern England where beech is plentiful

in 1902 and still flourishes in the counties of Buckingham, Bedford and Hertford in the triangle of country between Aylesbury, Luton and High Wycombe. These large, squirrel-like dormice feed mainly on fruit and nuts and in autumn hibernate in hollow trees. But sometimes they get into the roofs or attics of houses where their scuttlings, before they settle down for their winter sleep, often lead people to think they are invaded by rats. A favourite item of diet is the beech mast (or nut) which is also avidly sought by many other animals. Unfortunately 'mast years' when the nuts are really plentiful only come at irregular intervals, usually following a long, warm summer. In the years between when no nuts are produced the animals have to look for other foods.

Special beechwood birds are almost as hard to think of as beechwood mammals but the one that perhaps best qualifies is the wood warbler. On the Continent its habitat is described in the *Atlas of European Birds* by K. H. Voous as 'predominantly beechwoods with an accessible ground covering of mosses, low grasses and herbage; also woods of large oak trees with an undergrowth of brambles and ferns but without a thick growth of shrubs . . .' In Britain not every beechwood has wood warblers, but many do; and it is noticeable that if there is a solitary beech among oaks, a pair of wood warblers often chooses to nest by it. On the other hand there are upland woods of sessile oak and birch that have many wood warblers with never a beech in sight. What all such woods have in common with beechwoods is a scarcity of thick undergrowth. This lack of a shrub layer and the sparseness of the field layer make beechwoods generally unattractive to nesting birds.

If autumn brings a mast year things can liven up considerably. Then the seed eaters may arrive in force, many of them chaffinches and bramblings from north Europe, feeding all day on the floor of the wood, often all nervously rising into the trees. That is the moment to see the white rump of the bramblings which distinguishes them from the chaffinches. The brambling's harsh nasal call, *zweek*, is also unmistakable. Otherwise, when they are all feeding together on a brown carpet of leaves, they can be hard even to see, let alone identify. In some districts a much rarer species, the hawfinch, also feeds on beech mast. It is a shy and furtive bird and difficult to observe, but once you have found a beechwood where it feeds you will find it there day after day. If a road runs by the wood your best chance of a close view

The brambling arrives from Scandinavia in October and lives on beech nuts when available

of a hawfinch is from a car, for birds and animals are much less nervous of people in vehicles than of people walking.

Beech is a temperate climate tree: on the Continent it does not grow in the far north, and in the south it grows mainly on the cooler uplands. When young it will thrive for many years in the deep shade of the parent trees and there it is happily sheltered from the worst of the frosts. For this reason young beeches in plantations are best grown under the protection of other trees which can act as 'nurses'. Beech attains its full magnificence after about 120 years but, if not felled, may go on twice that long. It is a tree well loved for the delicate spring green of its unfolding leaves, the coolness of its summer shade, the glory of its autumn reds and yellows, the fine tracery of its winter twigs. We admire its colonnades of trunks within the forest for their architecture. Just as striking are the fascinating shapes of holes and branches in anciently pollarded beeches that must surely have inspired some modern sculptors.

One last word: the soft, thin bark looks so much like a parchment it often tempts people to carve their names. But this is terribly bad for the tree: it not only disfigures its smooth beauty, it can also let in the spores of harmful fungi which may do great damage.

CHAPTER 8

BIRCHWOODS

BIRCH is a tough little tree. If you were to go on a journey from Central
Europe to Lapland you would pass through several different types of
forest – beech, oak, spruce – but the very last forests of all, facing some
of the world's coldest weather near the edge of the open tundra,
would be mere patches of mixed birch and conifer scrub, for many of
the trees that struggle to survive there never exceed half a metre in
height. In north Canada or north Siberia you would find the same: for
birch forest is circumpolar. Birch is not only tough, it is also versatile,
for it grows all over the temperate zone as well as in the far north. So if
you live in south-east England you will probably know of birchwoods
quite near your home for there are plenty of them, especially on sandy
soils, in Surrey, Kent, Sussex; and many other counties elsewhere in
England. In colder regions, birch makes climax forest. But in the mild
climate of England and Wales a birchwood is usually impermanent. It
may start life when its seed gets blown on to an area of waste land or the
site of a felled or burnt woodland. As it grows up the birchwood
usually gets invaded by oaks as jays bring along the acorns and bury
them. Eventually the birches get overgrown by the oaks (or possibly
beeches) and the birchwood is smothered out of existence. So any
birchwood you know in England or Wales, unless it is being deliberately kept as a birchwood, is probably on its way to becoming a different
sort of wood altogether, provided it is protected from grazing.

But though birch never seems to form climax forest in England and
Wales and is often a stage in the formation of an oakwood, things are
different in the Scottish Highlands. There the birch is much less chal-
lenged by other species and there are many large birchwoods which
certainly look like climax woods. Most of them clothe steep hillsides but
some grow on level or rolling terrain. The best Scottish birchwoods,
according to an expert on the subject, Dr D. N. McVean, are in the
Lochinver-Drumbeg area of Assynt; the Torridon-Kishorn region;
lower Glen Affric; the south-east shore of Loch Ness; Deeside and
Strathspey; Morrone, Braemar; and the north and south shores of
Loch Rannoch. Behind the town of Aviemore, Inverness-shire, is a
National Nature Reserve called Craigellachie which has a particularly

attractive birchwood round a lake. But all birchwood is beautiful especially in the sunlight of late winter when the twigs glow with a rich purple-red – so lovely against the snowy hillsides.

Most British foresters regard birch as a weed. It is often felled to make room for conifers which grow well on the birchwood's acid soils. So it is fortunate for our landscape that birch is an eager coloniser for it means that though birches disappear from one place, other birchwoods are quick to spring up wherever they get the chance. They would by now cover great tracts of Scotland's semi-uplands if their adventurous seedlings were not severely controlled by moor-burning, which is a systematic firing of old heather and grassland to encourage the new young growth important in the diet of grouse, sheep and cattle. So by felling and burning, grazing by animals and nibbling by rodents the Scottish birch forests are kept within bounds. In fact they are presumably on the retreat, a fact which is deplored even by some foresters who argue that if treated with the lavish care now given to foreign conifers the birch could produce far more timber than it does at present. Birch enthusiasts argue that we should not judge Scotland's birchwoods by the dwarfed, twisted, unhappy-looking trees that so many of them now consist of, because these woods are the products of neglect. They claim that by growing the best strains and properly caring for their cultivation Scottish birchwoods might equal the fine birchwoods of Sweden where the tree is a most valuable national resource in great demand at home and for export.

Three species of birch are recognised as native in Britain: silver birch, downy birch and dwarf birch. This last is a very local arctic-alpine shrub which in Britain is found only in the Scottish uplands. At most it grows a metre in height. So it is only the other two birches which form woodlands. Both are common and widespread in Britain but the downy birch, because it can cope with wetter, colder soils, is most abundant in Scotland, Ireland and Wales, especially on high ground. Silver birch grows best on lighter, drier soils except that it usually avoids chalk. But the habitat differences between the two birches are not very pronounced. There are woods of silver birch and woods of downy birch both in the Scottish Highlands and in the south of England. Both silver and downy birches are commonest on acid soils. So when they are replaced naturally by oak it is usually by sessile oak. Probably before man interfered with the forests of Scotland, the normal pattern was sessile oak up the lower slopes merging into a belt of birch-pine forest higher up, the birches being mostly downy birches. This pattern is still to be seen here and there on Scottish mountainsides.

PLATE II. *Above*, in the adult stage, shown here, the cockchafer eats the leaves of trees, sometimes causing great damage. When very abundant its underground larvae are equally destructive of the roots of plants and trees. *Below*, the tanner beetle (*Prionus coriarius*) is the largest of British long-horn beetles. It is found in the southern half of England.

PLATE 12. Woodland moths. *Above left*, the large emerald, a beautiful green moth, is widespread in woodlands and also on heaths. *Right*, the leopard is commonest in south-east England and the Midlands; its caterpillar burrows into branches of many kinds of tree. *Below*, very variable, the peppered moth is often quite black, especially in industrial areas where it is well camouflaged as it rests on smoke-blackened tree-trunks.

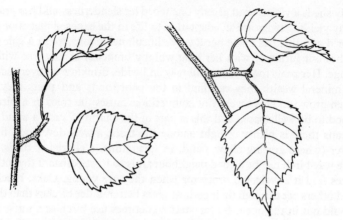

Left, downy birch; *right,* silver birch. They are frequent colonisers of cleared woodlands on acid soils

But more commonly, birch and sessile oak grow mixed in the woods of Highland Britain and are spoken of as birch-oak woods.

Silver birch and downy (or hairy) birch, though separate species, are much alike. But even at a distance two differences will often, but not always, pick them out. One is the extra-brilliant whiteness of the silver birch's bark; the other is that silver birch branches usually droop at the tips (hence the specific name *pendula* which means hanging). More precise differences are that silver birch has hairless twigs which have pale little warts on them whereas downy birch twigs lack the warts and are usually covered with short hairs (hence the specific name *pubescens* which means downy). The shape and toothing of the leaves also distinguishes the species. In silver birch the leaf is sharply pointed and has some teeth longer than the rest, the longer ones often curving in towards the leaf tip. Downy birch leaves are less pointed and the teeth, which are more or less equal, are not so prominent as those of silver birch. There are other less dependable differences but one thing is certain: there is no mistaking a really fine mature silver birch – it makes a taller tree (up to 25 m.) than the downy birch (20 m.) and its whole bark (except the rough lower part of the trunk) shines magnificently silver-white. This, therefore, is the species preferred for planting in parks and gardens.

The beauty of birches has often inspired the poets. James Russell Lowell, for instance, called the tree 'most shy and ladylike'. Gardeners and foresters, however, know that though the birch may be a lissom

lady she is a vicious and greedy one too. Her slenderness and her grace-
fully yielding twigs are an adaptation to life in the exposed places of the
world and this has made her a very difficult neighbour, for in a gale she
lashes out furiously with her long whippy branches at any tree within
range. Her roots too spread shallowly and wide, drinking up every scrap
of mineral wealth they can find in the poor sands and peats they so
often grow in. This severity of competition causes the trees in a birchwood to be well spaced and this is part of the charm of such a wood. It
means there is plenty of light among the trees, a well developed field
layer (where grazing allows) and, in springtime, a chorus of birds. In
one way birch can be a good neighbour: it is so frost-resistant that other
trees find it a welcome protector when they are young. Oaks, beeches
and others get through their earliest years better under birches than they
would out in the open. So foresters sometimes use birch as a nurse for
more delicate species, cutting the birch out after a few years when the
other trees are past their tenderest years.

Birchwoods are not famous for a wealth of wildflowers or shrubs: the
nitrogen-deficient soils on which most of them grow are acceptable to
very few species. And the incessant grazing by sheep, cattle and deer is
often a further depressing influence on the flora. But if you visit a
Scottish birchwood that is protected from animals, as happens in the
nature reserve at Aviemore, you will find a good development of grasses
and attractive plants such as petty whin (yellow gorse-like flowers) and
chickweed wintergreen (delicate white flowers like those of wood
anemone). In some birchwoods the ground may be thick with shrubs of
bilberry, or with juniper as in Morrone Wood near Braemar. An extreme type of habitat is that of high-level birchwoods and birch-oak-
woods which have developed on mountainside block scree. There the
ground layer is triumphant – a riot of mosses and lichens in all shades of
green which not only covers every great slab and chunk of rock but
forms a shaggy green jacket round every tree and out along many a
branch. In contrast, lower down the valleys on brown, mineral-rich
soils you will find birchwoods with quite a prosperous shrub layer of
hazel and under it a profusion of violets, wood anemones and that little
white umbellifer, the pignut.

Splendid fungi grow in birchwoods. In the birch zone of the Continent and Russia fungi are eagerly collected and stored as winter food.
Many species are eaten and the people there become highly skilled at
distinguishing the palatable ones from those which are inedible or
poisonous. But in Britain where because of the mild climate there is no
tradition of laying in stores of winter food hardly anyone ever eats

Boletus scaber, a large toadstool typical of birchwoods where it lives in intimate association with the tree roots

woodland fungi. The fly agaric is our best known birchwood fungus because it is big and brilliantly coloured (red cap usually with white spots) and often grows in large groups. Unfortunately it is poisonous. It is one of the toadstools whose underground part (mycelium) lives in mycorrhizal association with the birch roots. *Boletus scaber,* distinctive with its brown cap, pale below and its tall, black-scaled, white stem, is another common birchwood species. Like some other mycorrhizal toadstools it is said to vary slightly according to the species of tree with which it is associated. Other birchwood toadstools include *Lactarius turpis* (cap dark yellow-brown and slimy), *Lactarius glyciosmus* (small with pale lilac cap and stem), *Russula aeruginea* (green cap, white stem), and a fair number of others. Besides toadstools, which can mostly be reckoned among the birch's allies, there are certain woody bracket fungi which are highly destructive, the chief one being the familiar birch bracket, *Polyporus betulinus,* which begins as a round white knob on the bark and develops into a large thick plate. Usually there are only one or two on a tree but occasionally you will see a birch bristling all over with them. These fungi live for many years and eventually kill the tree. In the north of Scotland another bracket, the amadou fungus, *Fomes fomentarius,* can also be found on birch. As each year it adds a new layer of spore-bearing tubes some old specimens grow to be really massive.

The oak forest which covered so much of Dark Ages Britain probably yielded to beech in the chalk districts, ash on the harder limestones,

alder in the swamps and pine in central and east Scotland. On much
high ground all over the British Isles, oak was probably defeated by
birch so successfully that birchwoods may well have been the most
extensive type of forest in all Britain except for oak itself. In any event,
birch has always been a vastly abundant tree and therefore it is natural
that a large number of insects has become adapted to life in birchwoods.
Take moths for instance: the caterpillars of 120 or more species of
moths have been found feeding on birch, a figure that is exceeded only
by oak. Of course most of these species feed on other trees as well,
especially oak, but some are almost exclusive to birch.

The group known as the thorn moths are characteristic of birchwoods. Several are yellowish and of fair size and often flutter about car
headlights if you stop near roadside trees. Their caterpillars are loopers
and when at rest can look very much like twigs. Another very twig-like
caterpillar is that of the peppered moth which you may find common in
birch and other woods. A biologically famous moth this. It is usually

Peppered moths. The black variety is found in industrial areas where
it is camouflaged for resting by day on sooty and grimy surfaces. The
caterpillar feeds on various trees including birch and oak

mainly white with black speckling and so is well camouflaged when it
rests by day on the pale trunks of birches and other trees. But in the
past century or so, where the tree trunks have become blackened by
smoke in industrialised districts, most peppered moths have also
turned black and so continue to be camouflaged. This is the classic
example of 'industrial melanism' and is extremely interesting to the
student of evolution and genetics. It was first noted in Manchester in
1850 but since then has been reported from most other smoky districts.
Whether the setting up of smokeless zones is going to turn all the
peppered moths white again remains to be seen, but there are signs
that this is beginning to happen. Industrial melanism (the name
comes from a Greek word meaning black) has affected a number of
other species besides the peppered moth.

A moth well camouflaged to survive amid birchwood greenery, is the
large emerald, a common and beautiful species which hides by day

PLATE 13. Woodland butterflies. *Top,* the silver-washed fritillary visits bramble flowers in July and August; its caterpillar lives on violet leaves. *Centre,* the speckled wood is on the wing all spring and summer, especially in woodland rides and clearings. It lays its eggs on grasses. *Below,* the white admiral, whose caterpillars feed on honeysuckle, is found mainly in woods of south and east England.

PLATE 14. Caterpillars of moths. *Above left,* usually found on birch, the Kentish glory caterpillar is bright green with creamy stripes. *Right,* the privet hawk-moth larva, which feeds also on ash leaves, grows to three inches and is green with purple and white stripes. *Below left,* when disturbed, the caterpillar of the sycamore moth coils up and looks as threatening as possible. *Right,* the eyed hawk caterpillar often rests like this during the day and feeds (on willow or apple) chiefly by night.

among the leaves. Its caterpillar is even more disguised: it is reddish-brown when small and hibernates close to a birch bud which it resembles. Then in spring when it starts to eat the leaves again it turns green to camouflage itself among them. Among other typical birch-wood moths are: the grey birch (well camouflaged against the pale bark), various prominents and hook tips, common white wave, yellow horned (whose caterpillar folds a birch leaf over to make a tent), orange underwing (a sunlight flier of early spring), the very local angle-striped sallow (mainly in the north-east Midlands and the Scottish Highlands). The Scottish Highland birchwoods are also the habitat of the Rannoch sprawler, a rarity found in Perthshire and Inverness-shire and remarkable in that it has been known to stay eight years in the chrysalis stage. (That was in confinement: whether it does this in natural conditions is unknown.) A more widespread species found in Scottish woods is the great brocade, an all-grey moth whose larvae feed on bog myrtle, birch and other leaves. The badly named Kentish glory is not a Kentish moth at all: it is only local in England, absent from Wales and Ireland and is best known in parts of Scotland. It is a fine, fast-flying, sunlight-active species whose habits resemble the emperor moth's in that the males are attracted over far distances to the freshly-emerged females on early spring days. The interesting group of moths called the clearwings (they look more like wasps than moths) are represented in birchwoods by the large red-belted clearwing (whose black body has a bright red band across it) and by the Welsh clearwing. The grub-like

Large red-belted clearwing moth.
Its larvae feed under birch bark

larvae of both these clearwings live in rotten birch stumps. No butter-fly belongs to birchwoods in the sense that its caterpillar eats birch leaves in preference to any others. But the chequered skipper is known to live in birchwoods near Fort William, Inverness-shire (its caterpillars live on woodland grasses).

Other insects common in birchwoods include the birch shieldbug; and the interesting parent bug which does something insects very rarely do (though which spiders often do) – the female protects her

w.

eggs while they lie on the underside of a birch leaf and, later, her young while they feed on birch catkins. Birch leaves neatly cut in half and rounded into tubes usually contain larvae of the birch leaf-roller weevil. Other leaves may be found with pale patches or lines on them: these are due to burrowing by the larvae of tiny moths and flies which eat the leaf tissues. Among galls on birches are two which are caused by mites: one species causes the buds to swell and die like the infamous 'big bud' disease of black currants; another mite causes those big untidy birds'-nest-like bunches of twigs called 'witches' brooms'. Some fungi are also known to cause witches' brooms on birch and other trees.

No vertebrate animals or birds are peculiar to British birchwoods. But some of the larger birchwoods of Scotland are the habitat, regular or occasional, of such mammals as are characteristic of Highland woods in general, especially roe and red deer, fox, badger and wild cat. Among summer birds, chaffinches and willow warblers are extremely common in birchwoods right to the north of Scotland: other typical birds include coal, blue, great and long-tailed tits, tree pipits, robins and redstarts. In recent years the redwing has begun to breed in birch-woods in north Scotland. In winter all over Britain the minute and multitudinous seeds of the birch are eagerly sought by small finches, especially redpolls and siskins. The birds take them off the trees in autumn or seek them on the ground below in winter.

Because birch has, for a tree, only a short life – say about the same as our own – we can study the rise and decline of birch woodland more easily than that of long-lived trees. The conclusion is that in Britain birchwoods are rather fugitive, not occupying many sites for long. In support of this idea is the observation that though birch is an eager coloniser there is often little regeneration in the interior of the woods it forms even where grazing is excluded. So after half a century or so, the wood may be already declining. In this sense we can say that birch-woods are ephemeral not only because they are often a first step in re-colonisation by oak but also because they are probably always on the move anyway. For even when not invaded by other trees there is some evidence that, unable to replace themselves, their sites eventually revert to heather or grassland. Then sooner or later there may be a recolonisa-tion and the cycle begins again.

CHAPTER 9

ALDERWOODS

BIRCH and alder look very different from each other. Yet compare their catkins and you will see they are very much alike. And since the classification of flowering plants is based on flower structure it is not surprising to find that birch and alder are placed in the same family, the Betulaceae. Both male and female alder flowers, as in the birch, grow on the same tree and appear before the leaves. The male flowers are catkins up to six cm. long and hang in little clusters from the ends of twigs, shedding copious yellow pollen into the wind. The female catkins are only about one cm. long but extend half as much again to form the woody, cone-like seed-receptacles which remain on the tree long after the many little wingless seeds have fallen to the ground.

The abundance of ancient alder pollen preserved in peat shows clearly that as the climate got warmer but wetter in the Atlantic Period, causing pine to retreat, alder became one of the very commonest trees. As it likes its roots in water it must have found an infinite number of suitable habitats in the days when Britain was thick with forests and before any swamp had been drained by man. No doubt in those days the rivers were often impeded by fallen trees and flooded widely into the forests, causing vast permanent morasses. The result was that much of the most mineral-rich valley-bottom soils were permanently water-logged, producing conditions ideally suited to the alder. For alder

Alder leaves and flowers. The long male catkins will expand and hang in the breeze that will disperse the pollen. The round female catkins become hard and cone-like and contain tiny seeds eaten by redpolls, siskins, etc.

demands not only much water in its soil but also high fertility. Therefore man has always found it very profitable to reclaim alder-covered
ground: from it have been formed some of the richest farmlands of all.

When we look into the ecology of alder we see that it enjoys four
main types of habitat, all fairly or very wet. First, alders abound along
the banks of lakes, rivers and brooks sometimes to the virtual exclusion
of other trees, sometimes sharing the banks with ash, willow, wych
elm, oak and other species. In such a site the long, thin, red roots of the
alder are often visible streaming in the water where the bank has been
washed away. Second, alder occurs in damp-floored, fertile, lowland
woodlands whose dominant trees are usually ash or pedunculate oak.
Third, in Highland Britain, and especially in Wales and north-west
Scotland, alder grows commonly on hillsides watered by springs,
usually with sessile oak, ash and birch but sometimes making little
woods on its own. Fourth, it grows in fens which are too wet for most
other trees.

It is this fourth habitat that is most important because it is there that
we find the largest, fairly pure alderwoods, though they are the merest
fragments of the great alder forests of prehistory. And here it would be
well to understand just what is meant by 'fen'. For though in general
usage a fen may be any sort of wet place, for ecologists it has the restricted use of vegetation growing on peat saturated with lime-rich
water. So it contrasts with a bog, which is waterlogged peat that is
quite lime-deficient and acid. Inevitably the fertility-seeking alder
flourishes in fens but will not grow in extremely acid bogs. But round
the margins of bogs, where the influence of water draining off less acid
ground is felt, there is often a zone of vegetation to which ecologists have
given the name 'lagg' (the word is Swedish). In the lagg, because it is
less acid, a more fen-like vegetation develops including a scattering or a
whole wood of alders.

The conversion of valley-bottom alderwoods into cultivated land by
draining and felling goes far back in time for when men first became
farmers they no doubt soon learned where to find the most fertile soils.
So by the end of the Middle Ages, alderwoods were everywhere fragmentary except for a great spread of them which, amid a wilderness of
sedges, reeds, alder buckthorns and willows, still defied drainage in the
Fens of eastern England. Very little of those Fens were brought under
the plough until the seventeenth century but, from then on, reclama-
tion was rapid and the characteristic Fen vegetation, dominated by
alders, disappeared from wide areas. To-day small patches of alder carr,
as this type of woodland is called, survive here and there, as at Wicken

Fen, sixteen kilometres north-east of Cambridge. You will find the word 'carr', which is of Viking origin, in some place names in northern and eastern districts.

But the best surviving examples of alder carr are those round the Norfolk Broads, that series of reed-fringed lakes very popular for sailing and fishing near Great Yarmouth. Alder carr in the Broads has all the appearance of native woodland – a real jungle of trees young and old with even older trees lying dead and rotting among a riot of flowering plants and mosses. Alder is dominant but it shares the tree layer with ash and downy birch. Sallows, both the buckthorns and guelder rose form the upper shrub layer. Below them is often privet, spindle, hawthorn, black currant, red currant and gooseberry. The rich field layer is rough with great stools of the tussock sedge and there are usually quantities of yellow flag, meadowsweet, comfrey, hemp agrimony, bittersweet, marsh marigold, stinging nettle and marsh fern. In the moist cool air that goes with all this shading vegetation there is an abundance of mosses, liverworts and lichens on the trees.

Vegetation is seldom stable for long, and watery habitats especially are liable to change as man interferes with the drainage or nature intervenes in some other way. So, in any watery place, always ask yourself whether this stretch of water, this wet thicket, this patch of rushes and so on, looks fairly permanent or is it soon going to change into something else. Here is a typical succession: a pool is formed by the blocking of a stream through silting; reeds increasingly invade the pool until it becomes a complete reed-bed; the water gets shallower and the reeds are invaded by sallows and then by alders and birches. This carr condition may prove to be a climax, but sometimes the ground goes on getting drier and sooner or later birds bring along a few acorns. And the end of it all is an oakwood.

Mycorrhizal association between alders and at least four species of toadstool has been recorded. One of these fungi is *Lactarius cyathula* which is small and reddish and has a cap that becomes saucer-shaped. Another is *Gyrodon lividus*, a yellow-capped boletus with a dark-brown stem. The other two are *Lactarius lilacinus* and *Gyrodon rubescens*. Other fungi are less neighbourly to the alder, *Polyporus radiatus* for instance, a bracket red-brown above and paler below, which attacks the trunk and causes heart-rot. Besides its mycorrhizal relationships with fungi, alder also has an intimate partnership with a species of bacteria which inhabit little nodules on the tree's rootlets. These bacteria have the ability to derive nitrogen directly from the air that is in the soil and this they pass on to the alder, the bacteria receiving carbohydrates in return. Because it gets atmospheric nitrogen in this way, the alder presumably needs to take that much less nitrogen from the soil and so helps to maintain the soil's fertility.

As the alder has been such an abundant tree for thousands of years, it has inevitably become host to legions of insects. But though its leaves, twigs and wood are attacked by a number of small beetles, saw-flies and something like fifty species of larger moths (not to mention the smaller), yet the sum of their damage is not usually great. Among the many moths we may note the white-barred clearwing, dingy shell, May high-flier, alder kitten and the conformist as particularly addicted, in the larval stage, to alder leaves. But the so-called alder moth has no more connection with alders than it has with several other trees for you may find its strange caterpillar (banded yellow and black with long clubbed hairs on either side of its body and nearly always holding its head turned towards its tail) on many different sorts of leaves. A number of insects living on alder feed also on birch, no doubt because of the long association of these two trees in carr habitats.

Like the alder moth, the so-called alder fly (*Sialis lutaria*) is not really connected with alders: this is a very common, brownish, prominently veined, sluggish fly usually seen crawling on waterside vegetation including alders in May and June. Its larvae inhabit underwater mud. Little red swellings clustered on alder leaves are galls caused by a mite called *Eriophyes laevis*.

What birds you will find in alderwoods depends on what sort of alderwood and what time of year it is. An alder carr in Norfolk can be a habitat for a large population of woodland and marsh birds attracted there by the variety of cover and the wealth of aquatic and woodland insects. Redpoll, sedge warbler, grasshopper warbler, nightingale, turtle dove, marsh tit, mallard and woodcock are likely to be nesting

The siskin breeds mainly in conifer forests but is more widespread in winter

along with birds that are common to most English woodlands. In Scotland you may hear the distinctive song of that newcomer, the redwing, not only in birches but also in lakeside alderwoods. In autumn and winter alders everywhere are a very favourite haunt of redpolls and siskins; these acrobatic little finches can often be watched at close range pecking the little seeds out of their cases. Seed falling into water from overhanging alders is eagerly accepted by mallard and teal.

One mammal is particularly associated with the alder because both share the same riverside world – the otter. It is often among the roots of an alder that the female otter has her earth and rears her young, an earth that may be quite invisible to us because it is entered from below water level. Otters, alas, have lately become scarce in many areas, a decline that is almost certainly due to poisonous insecticides and other pollutants getting into streams. Otters live where fish are common and the alder greatly helps the fish by casting welcome shade on the water, strengthening the river banks with its roots and dropping its seeds which many fish readily eat.

Though alder wood has had many past uses it has very few to-day except in north Europe where much of it goes for plywood. In Britain it was used until earlier this century for making the soles for clogs that were sent to Lancashire and neighbouring counties. To-day, because hardly anyone has any economic reason for having alderwoods on his land, they have become scarce and eventually hardly any will survive except in nature reserves. Fortunately the alders remain common in other habitats, especially watersides, where they are a beautiful adornment of the scene, notably in March when their red-purple catkins bring brilliant colour to many miles of lakeside and river.

CHAPTER 10

ASHWOODS

LOOKING up into an ash even at high summer, you see plenty of light coming down through the well spaced, pinnate leaves and shining on the pale smooth branches. A result of all this light that gets into an ash-wood is that there are often well developed shrub, field and ground layers. But what species you will find there depends on the sort of ground the wood is growing on.

Let us begin with a common type of ashwood which, far from being purely of ash, is best described as an oak-ashwood. This sort of wood was probably once a coppice of ash with standard trees of pedunculate oak. But then it got neglected and the result was a multitude of young ash trees growing from the coppiced stools as well as from seedlings. In the course of time these young ashes thinned each other out by com-

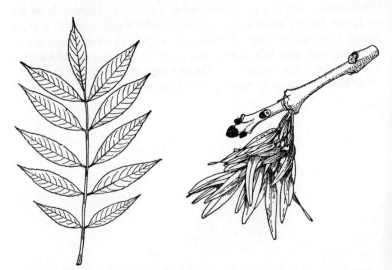

Ash leaf and fruits. This is one leaf, not eleven. Leaves so divided into leaflets are called pinnate. Winged fruits are known as samaras, each of which holds a seed in its base

petition, leaving the strongest to grow up and outnumber the oaks as mature trees. If you know a wood of this kind you can be pretty sure of two facts about its soil: it will be fairly damp at all seasons and it will be mostly lime-rich underneath even if not right at the surface. Of these two factors the lime-richness is the most important in the victory of the ash. For oak can flourish as well as ash on a damp rich loam. But an extra bit of lime in the soil seems often to tip the balance in favour of ash.

The shrub, field and ground layers in an oak-ashwood can be very rich in species. Both oak and ash, especially ash, come into leaf late in spring which means a great flush of those woodland flowers which appear in the first third of the year in order to avoid the shades of summer. Then follow the summer-flowering, or aestival, species which can stand the gentle shade cast by the ash. Add to these influences the water always percolating through the ground, the wealth of available minerals in the loam, and you have a flora that can be more varied than that of any other type of British woodland.

In such a wood the shrub layer may, at first glance, look no different from that of an average lowland oakwood, for it will consist mostly of hazel and young ash, with a scatter of field maple. But among the very common species you may well find some which are less generally distributed in Britain because they demand a limy soil, shrubs such as dogwood, privet, spindle and, especially in southern England, wayfaring tree. The field layer, in addition to quantities of normal damp oakwood wildflowers such as dog's mercury and enchanter's nightshade, is likely to include ramsons, drooping sedge, nettle-leaved bellflower, hairy St John's wort, herb Paris, wood dog violet and many others. A special plant of this type of woodland is the oxlip (see page 36). In the ground layer will be many mosses characteristic of limy soils. Dead ash branches lying about (or on the trees) are likely to have shiny black knobs on them – the fungus called King Alfred's cakes (*Daldinia concentrica*). Ash apparently has no mycorrhizal associations with fungi.

Because for centuries oak has been the great house-building, shipbuilding and general purpose tree, man has encouraged it at the expense of other species, allowing just enough ash to mature to satisfy the needs of craftsmen who wanted it for special jobs such as farming tools and carts. Whether large tracts of more or less pure ashwoods ever developed on the fertile lowland soils of prehistoric Britain is not known. What seems most likely is that mature ash was originally much commoner in the ancient oakwoods than it is in many present-day oakwoods.

If, instead of oak-ashwoods you want to see pure ashwoods, you had best go to chalk or limestone districts, for except in the beechwood area of southern England and Wales, ash is the typical climax tree of very calcareous ground. To see the biggest and most natural ashwoods go to the Mendips or the Pennines. In those evidently ancient woods the ash grows practically unchallenged by other trees because it is the species best able to tolerate the shallow, very alkaline soils that exist on the Carboniferous Limestone. Not that ash grows all that well in such circumstances; the trees of these limestone woods are often of poor growth, nothing to compare with the magnificent ashes you can see on rich, lowland soils. In this the limestone ashes resemble the mis-shapen sessile oaks of acid mountainsides: for those oaks too would make far better growth on richer soils.

Ashwoods on limestone may not yield any timber but they are highly valued by naturalists as the habitat of many distinguished species of our flora and fauna. The shrub layer may include plenty of hawthorn, hazel and wild roses; and smaller quantities of dogwood, spindle, common buckthorn, privet and elder. The Mendip ashwoods also have traveller's joy and wayfaring tree. The plants of the field

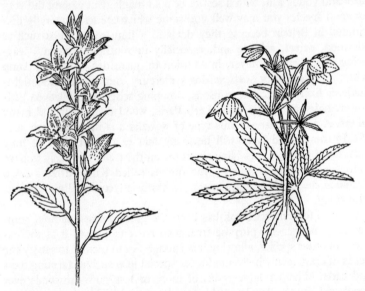

Left, giant bellflower; *right,* green hellebore. Giant bellflower grows mainly in northern woodlands. Green hellebore is very local in southern lime-rich woods

layer consist of numerous species such as sweet woodruff, early purple orchid and dog's mercury which characterise damp, base-rich woodlands generally. But in addition there are many which are far more local such as giant bellflower, columbine, globe flower, Jacob's ladder and green hellebore.

One of the most remarkable limestone ashwoods in Britain is Colt Park Wood, a National Nature Reserve at 335 m. altitude in the Pennines on the slopes of Ingleborough, a mountain famous for its lime-loving species. The wood grows on what is called limestone pavement; that is, a more or less level platform of rock which in the course of ages has become deeply fissured so that it now consists of huge flat blocks of limestone with deep wide cracks (locally called 'grikes') between them. Some of these grikes are wide enough to walk in and are deeper than a man is tall. In them and all over the blocks of limestone (which are mostly covered with shallow black soil) there is a riot of trees, shrubs, flowering plants, ferns and mosses. The trees are ash with a sprinkling of wych elms. There is a copious shrub layer of hazel, hawthorn, bird cherry and blackthorn. But it is the field layer that is most splendid, a luxurious riot of flowering plants and ferns showing every sign of enjoying life in the cool dampness of the grikes. Ferns include hartstongue and rigid buckler, moonwort and a little green spleenwort. Among the commoner flowering plants are fine, tall red campions, much birdseye speedwell and sweet woodruff, a fair amount of shining cranesbill, wood anemone and lesser meadow rue. Choicer plants include baneberry, a curious member of the buttercup family, half a metre or so in height with feathery white flowers and found in Britain only on these northern limestones; lily of the valley, angular Solomon's seal, herb Paris, melancholy thistle, yellow star of Bethlehem, northern hawksbeard and many other interesting species. Limestone mosses abound.

Herb Paris is found locally in woods on dampish limy soils

Apart from sheer cliffs, Colt Park Wood is the most hazardous place I know for naturalists. It is extremely easy to stumble in that multi-fissured terrain. So if you go there, take care. Because of these dangers sheep and cattle are excluded, which goes far to explain why the plant life is so abundant.

Another noteworthy limestone ashwood (also a National Nature Reserve) is Rassal Wood on a hillside in Wester Ross, Scotland, a mile north of Loch Kishorn along A896. Its value to the naturalist is two-fold: first, it is Britain's most northerly ashwood and it is interesting to be able to see how well the ash grows at its highest latitude; second, having been grazed mercilessly for years by sheep, deer, hares and rabbits it was, until it became a reserve, a dying wood with no hope of young trees coming on. But since 1957 a few acres of the wood have been protected from grazing by a fence and to-day you can see the wood reconstructing itself into its four proper layers: the tree layer of old, past-their-best ashes will eventually be replaced by the young ashes springing up vigorously for the first time for perhaps two centuries; a shrub layer is already well developed with hazel, rowan, willow, bird cherry and a little birch and guelder rose. The field layer too is dra-matically rich compared with the short grazed turf outside the wood-land fence: there is a fine growth of bluebells, primroses, wood anem-ones, herb Robert, water avens and many grasses; and a profusion of calcicole mosses on the woodland floor. Rassal ashwood is, without a doubt, a woodland saved at the eleventh hour.

Twelve kilometres north-east of Dolgellau in Meirionydd, north Wales, there is another sort of ashwood, one that has sprung up not on sedimentary limestone but on a limestone of igneous origin, for this was a volcanic region 400 million years ago. The ancient lava has broken up to form a rough loose scree on a hillside called Craig y Benglog. On part of this slope grows a straggling old ashwood, and under the trees and just outside the wood there are many lime-loving plants such as rock arabis, rockrose, early purple orchid, marjoram, rock stonecrop and lesser clubmoss, species which are rare or quite absent in the surrounding countryside because of its limeless soils. Ashwoods on sedimentary limestone are rare in Wales but the mixed gorge-side woods of south-west Brecon are very rich in ash and there is a pure ashwood with many calcicole plants on the cliff called Craig y Rhiwarth, a reserve of the Brecknock County Naturalists' Trust in the Tawe valley, an area famous for its vast cave systems.

So far we have looked at fairly natural oak-ashwoods on damp, base-rich soils and quite natural pure ashwoods on limestone. There is another habitat where ash is common but is nearly always accompanied by other trees. This is where the soil, though fairly acid, is mineral-rich and copiously supplied with water that is draining quickly through it. These conditions exist on river banks (where the ash is often growing with oak, alder and wych elm) and on hillsides where moisture is trickling down. So a sessile oakwood growing along the flank of a hill may have a row of ash growing down it wherever a drainage line comes down the woodside. In such gullies and hollows the soil is enriched with minerals carried into them by the percolating water. Whether this sort of ash which likes its feet near running water belongs to a different variety from the ash that grows in dry limestone is not certain: but German botanists have suggested that two such types of ash do exist which they call 'limestone ash' and 'water ash'.

If you look at the foliage of an ash at midsummer you will soon see that, compared with oak and birch, fewer insects are in the habit of eating it. True, thirty or so different moth caterpillars (of the Macrolepidoptera) have been found on ash but very few have a special preference for it. Among those which have is a beautiful moth called the centre-barred sallow, the 'centre bar' being a purple band across the orange-yellow wing. It is a nocturnal late-summer moth whose caterpillar feeds, also at night, as soon as the ash buds begin to open in spring. It is recorded from many parts of the British Isles. Another species exclusive to ash is the coronet moth, a much drabber species, widely distributed except in Ireland; it flies about midsummer and the caterpillar is to be looked for a month or so later. Ash is related to lilac and privet (they are members of the olive family) and presumably their leaves taste somewhat alike because several caterpillars feed on all three. Best known perhaps is the privet hawk, a large and magnificent bright-green, purple-striped caterpillar which is commonest in the south of England. Another sizeable caterpillar, that of the goat moth, does not eat ash leaves but burrows into its trunk (it attacks elm, birch and other trees too). Eating slowly into the solid wood it tunnels along near the surface for several years before it pupates. You may find a tree which has large goat-moth holes in its trunk. If so it is worth remembering and revisiting on a warm summer or autumn day because these holes have a long-lasting, peculiar smell attractive to red admiral butterflies. I once saw twenty-two red admirals all crowded round a group of goat-moth holes on an ash trunk. You might think the goat-moth larva, living inside wood, should be safe from all enemies. Yet there is a big ichneumon fly (*Lampronata setosa*) which, using its acute sense of smell, can locate the goat-moth caterpillar from the

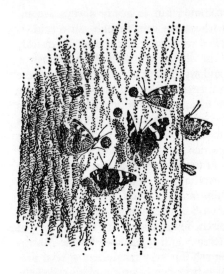

Red admirals round goat-moth burrows on an ash trunk. They and other insects are attracted by the sap that exudes from these holes

outside of the bark. It then pierces the tree with its hard, very sharp ovipositor and lays an egg on or near the body of the caterpillar, which is eventually devoured by the ichneumon larva.

Ashwoods, especially those on limestone, are the habitat of many interesting calcicole insects but do not seem to have any special verte-brates. Small rodent mammals are often abundant in the leaf-litter especially of the oak-ashwoods for there they may enjoy a varied diet of acorns and ash seeds, particularly the latter, for ash produces seeds copiously nearly every year, far more reliably than oak. One bird which certainly likes the ash in spring is the wood pigeon: it gobbles up the purple flowers with obvious relish.

We can regard ash as a typical temperate climate tree; and though woods of ash are not very common, individual ash trees grow naturally all over Britain except on mountains and at the northern extremities of the Scottish mainland. On the Continent, ash grows only as far north as the southern quarter of Norway; and in the south it is absent from the Mediterranean region except on the cool mountains. In other words it avoids the extremes of heat and cold. It can suffer damage in a severe winter. In spring it is usually the last tree to venture into leaf. In autumn it sheds its leaves quite early, sometimes when still green though often they turn a lovely pale yellow. Then the brown 'keys', as its winged seeds are called, hang in conspicuous bunches from the twigs and it may be months before they are scattered by the wind. In the forests of the Middle Ages, when timber was so common and cheap, trees were valued mainly for the food they provided for the many herds of pigs; and because pigs do not eat ash keys until every acorn has gone, the ash had a very low rating. In the laws of the tenth century Welsh king Hywel Dda (Howell the Good) an oak was reckoned to be worth thirty times as much as an ash.

To summarise the place of ash in our woodlands: tolerant of thin, rocky, lime-rich soils and evidently needing plenty of summer rain and not enjoying excessive heat, ash can flourish on upland limestones of the north and west, both on hard fissured rock of pavements and also on screes. As no other large tree can cope with these conditions so success-fully ash is the dominant tree in such places. On fertile, damp soils of the lowlands, especially on deep loams, the ash grows extremely well but there it has to contend with the oak; and although perhaps in many woods ash was once commoner than oak, man has helped the oak to dominate the ash by selective felling. In the chalk woodland of south England conditions might seem right for the ash except that in most places the soil dries out too much in summer; so in these districts ash, though flourishing in pockets, seems more usually only a stage in the succession from scrub to beechwood.

CHAPTER II

SCOTS PINEWOODS

THE conifer known to science as *Pinus sylvestris* is widespread in Europe and has names in many languages. We call it the Scots pine because in Britain it is only in the Scottish Highlands that it is a native species forming natural woodlands. One of our loveliest trees, the Scots pine, when mature, has a richly red, loosely flaking bark which is gloriously colourful in the setting sun; and the blue-green foliage goes well with the redness of the boughs. It may grow to great size in about a century and develop huge spreading limbs worthy of any oak. For most of its life its shape is full and rounded but in its old age it usually becomes flat-topped. Of course to achieve a beautiful shape a pine, like any other tree, must grow without close competition. Where pines grow

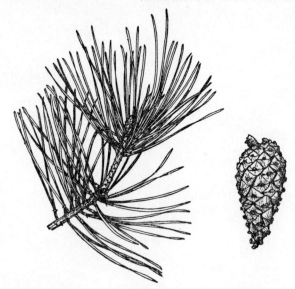

Scots pine leaves and cone. The leaves (needles) grow in pairs. The cones contain seeds (two under each scale) that are eaten by crossbills, squirrels etc.

PLATE 15. Wood borers. *Above,* the giant woodwasp (*Urocerus gigas*), a species of saw-fly, bores into hard wood to lay an egg inside it with her powerful, inch-long ovipositor. From the egg hatches a larva that lives on the wood as it burrows. But then along may come an ichneumon fly, *Rhyssa persuasoria* (*below*), that can locate the woodwasp larva by scent. She too drills through the wood, lays an egg on or near the woodwasp larva which is eventually eaten by the larva of the ichneumon fly.

PLATE 16. Wood ants. *Above,* large heaps of pine needles and other leaves in woods are nests of the wood ant, our largest species. *Below,* the ants can be seen scurrying over the ground and even high up trees, seeking and bringing back nest material and food to their colonies.

crowded together as in plantations they are more like tall poles with a small tuft of foliage on top.

Although Scots pine covered much of Britain before the Atlantic Period it eventually, as the climate got less cold, gave way to other trees until all that was left of real pine forest was in the Scottish Highlands where to-day it still forms large woods in a few places and reaches up mountainsides to 625 m. But though the pine forests shrank away northwards it seems reasonable to suppose that some pines survived here and there in south Britain and that their descendants are the lone pines we find scattered in broad-leaved woods in many places. Equally such isolated trees could be colonisers from the many Scots pinewoods planted in Britain over the past few hundred years. As this pine grows quickly and can flourish on poor soils it became a favourite tree to plant in southern Britain where the best land had long since gone for farming. It is so accommodating that it will grow both on chalk and on acid peat. But it is in sandy places particularly that there are extensive Scots pine plantations, especially in south-east England. In Surrey, for instance, there are attractive pinewoods in the north-west (on Bagshot sand) between Weybridge and the Chobham ridges; and farther south (on greensand) around Abinger, Leith Hill and Hindhead. Pine planta- tions, however, though they may enhance the Surrey landscape, are of limited interest as you soon realise when you get to Scotland and see natural pinewoods in all their beauty and splendour, and with their special fauna and flora intact.

From the Atlantic Period until about three centuries ago the natural place of much of the pine forest in Scotland may have been the ground intermediate in altitude between the oakwoods of the lower slopes and the birchwoods of the mountainsides. But so great has been the clear- ance of woodland since the seventeenth century that it is uncommon to find this zonation anywhere to-day, if indeed it ever existed. It is par- ticularly rare to find birch clearly zoned above pine for the two so often grow together, their soil and other requirements being closely similar. And in Rothiemurchus Forest, where there is the highest natural tree- line remaining in Britain, the last trees up the slopes are pines merging into a narrow zone of juniper scrub.

When the glaciers melted off the Highlands, they left many of the slopes deeply covered by coarse sands and gravels: it is these poor soils, especially at higher altitudes, which pine and birch have colonised to the exclusion of most other trees, the soil requirements of birch and pine being easily satisfied. Both pine and birch are energetic colonisers whenever they get the chance. Their highly fertile seed is produced in abundance and is easily carried by the wind to fall in treeless places. But as I mentioned in Chapter 8 moor-burning and heavy grazing are powerful preventers of forests. Within the old Highland forest itself good regeneration is not very common but it is taking place in Rothiemurchus Forest, in nearby Abernethy Forest and a few other places. Research is proceeding into problems of pine re-generation at Beinn Eighe National Nature Reserve.

On the Continent the Scots pine is very widespread, some of its greatest forests being in Russia and Scandinavia (whence its timber is exported as 'Norway pine' and 'yellow deal'). On the Continent it grows best in the drier regions, so Continental foresters are surprised when they visit Britain and see it flourishing in our wet oceanic climate. Long isolated from the Continent, the pines of Scotland are reckoned to be a local race that has become adapted to the wetter climate.

Perhaps all you know of pinewoods is what you have seen in planta-tions where the rows and rows of trunks grow out of a deep soft layer of needles which smother nearly all the ground vegetation. If so the wild pinewoods of Scotland could be a delightful surprise for you. There the pines are of all ages and sizes, sometimes close to each other, sometimes with spaces and glades between. Despite all the felling, quite a few grand old specimens remain. And all the woods are set amid magnificent scenery of lakes, hill slopes and mountain peaks. Under these ancient pinewoods you will find thick carpets of bilberry, heather and crowberry and among them three plants which, without forming great mats, are nevertheless very common: tormentil, heath bedstraw and wavy hair-grass. Where the pines are large and growing close enough to each other to form a heavy canopy there is usually no real shrub layer apart from thinly scattered birches and rowans. But in clearings where full light gets into the forest there are often bushes, even whole thickets of juniper, some tall and upright, some low and strag-gling. Where pinewoods climb high up the slopes you may come to a zone where the ground is covered by great stretches of cowberry and bearberry, both members of the bilberry family. If you are a keen plant seeker you might be afraid that all these far-spreading species must be rather monotonous. But in fact the Scottish pinewoods are enlivened by the presence of several choice wildflowers, among them some of the loveliest and rarest in Britain. Notably there is the twinflower, or Linnaea, named after the great Swedish botanist Linnaeus (1707-78) who first gave us the scientific names of so many of our plants and animals. Linnaea is a small creeping species and has twin, delicate, drooping pink flowers. The pinewoods also have the coralroot orchid,

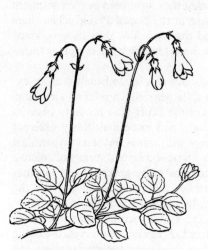

Twinflower (*Linnaea borealis*).
Named after the Swedish botanist, Linnaeus, it is a very local
plant of pine forests in eastern
Scotland

One-flowered wintergreen, a rarity of Scottish pinewoods

a yellowish plant which, like the birdsnest orchid of the beechwoods,
feeds directly on rotting vegetation instead of getting chemicals from
the soil. In other words, it is saprophytic. Another orchid, creeping
lady's tresses, has a spiral of little white flowers on a spike fifteen to
twenty cm. tall. A third orchid of the pinewoods, but which grows in
many other habitats, is the lesser twayblade, a plant often so small (it
may be no more than six cm.) that its tiny reddish spikes are hard to
spot. An outstandingly attractive plant is the one-flowered wintergreen which hangs a lone, usually down-facing, waxy flower about
nine cm. above the ground. There are four other wintergreens
with similarly beautiful flowers, all to be found here and there in the
pine forest. They are the greater, the round-leaved, the common and
the serrated wintergreens. Finally there is a much commoner plant than
these, the chickweed wintergreen which is also a species of the birchwoods. Its flower has 5-9 white petals, very dainty foliage and often
roots itself very lightly in leaf mould rather than in proper soil. (Wintergreen is a misleading name for this plant which is really a member of
the primrose family.) Most of these wildflowers, though so typical of
the Highlands, are also found sparingly scattered in various parts of

England and Wales. It is possible that they have been in their southern localities ever since they grew there in the Boreal Period when there were pine forests everywhere; and that somehow they have survived the changes of climate which have been too much for the pines themselves.

That pinewoods, like birchwoods, are rich in toadstools is to be expected once we realise that acid soils generally produce more fungi than basic soils do. Like most trees the Scots pine needs to have its root tips intimately linked with fungi and more than thirty different toadstools have been found living with pines in this mycorrhizal association; among them are the fly agaric and several species of boletus. In addition there are scores of fungi of many genera found in pinewoods without any known mycorrhizal functions. Some grow on the living trees and can do great harm by causing heart-rot: such is *Polyporus schweinitzii*, a large, velvety, red-brown toadstool on a short thick stem that grows at the base of the trunk. *Fomes annosus*, a ragged-looking bracket, brown above and light below, is another destroyer of pines and also spruces.

Though compared with that of oakwoods the number of pinewood insects is not great, they include some very well studied ones because of the high commercial value of the pine. There are several beetles which feed in the bark and the cambium. The large pine weevil strips the soft skins of young pine shoots. The black pine beetle attacks the trees at their roots. A very striking beetle is the timberman, one of the longhorn group. Its antennae are 8 cm. long (compared with a body of only 2 cm.) and trail behind when the beetles fly, which they do on warm days of early summer; the larvae burrow into pine timber, eating it as they go. The larvae of several sawflies live exclusively on conifer needles. Gall-mites cause swellings on young pine branches.

Among moths there are several small species whose larvae damage pine shoots by tunnelling inside them. The larger pinewood moths include a few defoliators such as the bordered white whose caterpillars

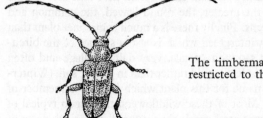

The timberman, a pinewood beetle restricted to the Scottish Highlands

PLATE 17. Catkins. *Above left,* male catkins of hazel extend and shake their pollen into the wind in winter and early spring to fertilise the tiny red female flowers. *Right,* silver birch catkins open later in spring than hazel. The female catkins are much smaller and more slender than the males and usually upright. *Below left,* "Pussy willow" is the name often given to sallow flowers; the male catkins, seen here on goat willow, are bright yellow with pollen when fully open. *Right,* alder in early autumn showing, left to right, next year's young catkins, this year's ripening fruits, and the remains of last year's cone-like fruit.

PLATE 18. Southern beechwood plants. Both the white helleborine (*above left*) and the birdsnest orchid (*right*) are commonest in beechwoods of southern England. The nettle-leaved bellflower (*below*) grows in beechwood clearings and margins (and other lime-rich habitats).

may do great damage in summer and autumn in pinewoods all over Britain: they are long and thin and green with white lines to match the needles among which they live. Also green with white lines are the caterpillars of the pine beauty, a moth which harmonises well with the reddish pine trunks. The Black Wood of Rannoch is a famous locality for the Rannoch looper, a little bright-chestnut moth whose caterpillars feed in spring on bilberry leaves and resemble bilberry twigs. An even smaller moth, the juniper pug, which is very variable in appearance, is found in the Highland forests as well as being widely ranging elsewhere in Britain. Another widespread juniper eater is the caterpillar of the juniper carpet moth.

Birds are very few in closely planted pinewoods. But in the native Scottish forests, though numbers are not great, there are some highly attractive species whose evolution is so tightly bound up with the Highland pine forest that they are now practically inseparable from it. Most striking are the crossbill and the crested tit, which are found nowhere else in Britain. The crossed mandibles of the crossbill are an adaptation enabling them to prise open the scales of cones to get at the seeds. The beak of the Scottish crossbill is especially large – a characteristic of those races of the crossbill which have evolved in pine forests as compared with races whose favoured habitat is spruce or larch forest (pine cones being harder to open than the others). These large-billed races are known as parrot crossbills and are regarded by some ornithologists as a separate species though apart from beak-size and habitat there is extremely little difference. Sometimes, usually in summer and autumn, there are invasions of Continental crossbills and for a while there are

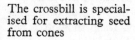

The crossbill is special-ised for extracting seed from cones

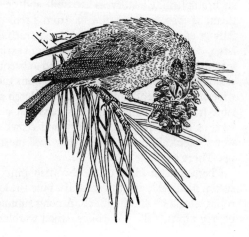

large-billed and small-billed crossbills in the Highland forests. But the two do not really mix; they are said to have a different call-note which helps to keep them apart.

The Scottish crossbill is an early nester, sometimes laying in February but usually in late March, building high up and out on the side branches of the pines and therefore hard to find. Its greatest numbers are in the Spey valley where large flocks form as soon as breeding is over; but it nests in other parts of the Highlands and adjacent districts, having colonised many pine plantations. It is forced by shortages of food to move from forest to forest because in any year the crop of pine seed may fail in some areas but succeed in others. Generally a Scots pine produces plenty of seed only every three or four years.

The crested tit likewise, having had its range severely reduced over the last three centuries by the clear-felling of the ancient forest, has benefited by the new pine plantations and extended its Scottish range this century, being now common on low ground near the east coast, along the lower Findhorn, for example. But it is far more restricted than the crossbill, its main centre still being the upper Spey valley as it has been for many years. There are thought to be 300-400 pairs now breeding in Scotland. Though it eats pine seed only occasionally, the crested tit is just as dependent on pine and spruce as the crossbill is: its food is mainly insects which it usually finds high up in the trees. As it does not migrate, the Scottish population of crested tits has been isolated for thousands of years and is now slightly different in appearance from the Continental race, being generally darker.

The pine forests' other special bird, the capercaillie, has not quite such a splendid history as crossbill and crested tit. For though, like them, it was in these forests from prehistoric times the wholesale fellings of recent centuries proved too much for it and this magnificent, large, dark-plumaged game bird became extinct about 1760. It was re-introduced from Sweden in 1837 and subsequent years, was able to re-establish itself in the new pine plantations then growing up and is now widespread in Scotland in spruce and larch as well as pine. Its food is varied: it eats mainly conifer shoots but also many kinds of berries such as rowan, juniper, bilberry and crowberry. Deep snow does not worry capercaillies: in winter they feed mostly in the trees, often high up. There too they roost.

Characteristic birds of the Scottish pinewoods in summer include siskin, goldcrest, great tit, coal tit, blue tit, long-tailed tit, tree creeper, robin, chaffinch and bullfinch. Among summer visitors there are plenty of tree pipits, willow warblers, wood warblers, spotted flycatchers and

Roe deer, a native species locally abundant and increasing in some British woodlands

redstarts. Mistle thrushes and wood pigeons are also plentiful. Commonest predator is the tawny owl, feeding on voles, wood mice and birds. There are also plenty of long-eared owls, a bird that might be heard by winter sports enthusiasts, for it calls very early in the year – a hoot about every two seconds produced with great regularity and sometimes going on for a long time. Buzzards and sparrow hawks are in fair numbers; and there are the now famous ospreys, a pair of which have in recent years been observed at the nest by thousands of people from a hide provided by the Royal Society for the Protection of Birds. Lakes amid forests are the osprey's most characteristic habitat in temperate regions. Exterminated by man over much of Europe (including the British Isles by 1908) it returned to breed in Scotland in the 1950s. Under protection it may, in time, thoroughly re-establish itself there near lakes abounding in fish, its almost exclusive food.

The most distinctive mammals of the Scottish woods are the roe and red deer. But neither is confined to woodland and certainly not to the ancient pinewoods. Of the two the roe is much the more wood-haunting though some are said to live on the moors far away from woods the whole year through. But in the pine forest the loud gruff bark of the roe is a characteristic sound and, where not persecuted, these deer have become approachable, feeding openly near trafficky roads in fields outside the forest. Young roe are born in the spring, usually twins. Until three months old they are prettily white-spotted, after which they become brown like the adults. The male roes fight a great deal in July and August, the rutting season.

The term 'deer forest' can deceive the uninitiated. Despite the name, a Scottish deer forest is not woodland but an area of treeless moorland and mountain, the typical habitat of red deer in Scotland. These tracts became deer forest in the nineteenth century when deer hunting had a great vogue. Till then many of them had been sheepwalks; since then some have become sheepwalks again. But red deer remain common and, especially the great antlered stags, are magnificent to see on the hills. One estimate of their population is that there are about 190,000 of them roaming over one and a half million hectares of the Scottish Highlands. The largest native British mammal, they normally seek lower ground in winter, a move which brings them into the habitat of roe deer in the old pine forests. With deer-stalking not as popular as formerly, the deer has rather fallen in favour. It is regarded as a pest by farmers and foresters who suffer from it in winter when deer easily cross high fences by walking on the crust of frozen snowdrifts. Roe are also disliked by the forester because they not only eat shoots but mark out their territories by fraying the bark off young trees. So both roe and red deer are selectively shot to keep down their numbers.

If its name were apt, the pine marten would be the most typical pine forest mammal. No doubt it was once, but unfortunately it has long

Pine marten, a member of the weasel family. It survives in a few woodland and mountain districts but is frequent only in and near the old Scottish pine forests

since become rare through persecution by gamekeepers and farmers and its habitat at present is mainly the wilder mountain country. But such a shy animal, largely nocturnal, could easily live in a pine forest without anyone realising it. Certainly pine martens are well known in the pinewoods of the Beinn Eighe National Nature Reserve and if you ever follow the splendid nature trail which goes through that reserve you should certainly keep an eye open for martens, for they are not nocturnal by preference, but only by necessity, so in the quiet of nature reserves they will probably become increasingly diurnal. Their commonest prey is reported to be the short-tailed vole. But they are supremely agile and can even run down squirrels in the tree tops.

The wild cat is a bigger, fiercer and altogether tougher animal than the domestic cat and has the reputation of being untameable even when taken from the wild as a kitten. Its general colour is pale tawny, darkly barred round its body and with dark rings on its bushy, blunt tail. It is locally not uncommon in the northern half of Scotland and has increased this century in the shelter of big conifer plantations. But being thoroughly disliked by farmers and gamekeepers, it is not likely to be allowed to spread far outside its haunts in the remoter forests and mountains. It eats many small mammals and birds and also mountain hare, rabbit and grouse. It is also said to take a few deer fawns and lambs.

Although the grey squirrel has spent most of this century spreading through south Britain and replacing the red squirrel nearly everywhere, it is noticeable that where there are extensive pine plantations the red

The red squirrel has decreased steadily this century and is now common only where the grey squirrel has not yet penetrated. It is characteristic of Scottish pine forests

squirrel tends to hold its own. So when the grey squirrel has spread as far as ever it can in Britain it seems likely that the pine forests of Scotland, both natural and planted, may remain a stronghold for the red squirrel. This squirrel, like the crossbill, feeds avidly on pine seeds, but whereas a 'crossbilled' cone has the scales bent back but not torn off, a 'squirrelled' cone is stripped bare of its scales. Neither squirrel is loved by foresters for both eat conifer shoots, so both are persecuted. Like the grey squirrel the red takes young birds from nests and when plentiful probably does quite a lot of damage among crossbills and other pinewood birds. With the spread of the grey squirrel across England and Wales this century and the fruitless campaign to control it there has arisen a popular belief that grey squirrels are pests but that red squirrels are harmless. So it comes as a surprise to many to be told that thousands of red squirrels have in the past been slaughtered as pests, especially in Scotland.

And now, which way to the natural pinewoods? All are in the northern half of Scotland, some north-west, some south-east of the Great Glen which cuts right across the country. You can find splendid pinewoods in Inverness-shire in Glen Affric, climbing up from the water's edge with the mountain called Mam Sodhail perhaps snow-capped above. Similar fine pinewoods climb from the shores of Loch Maree in Ross and Cromarty. Other well-known fragments of the old pine forest survive in the Black Wood of Rannoch on the slopes of Schiehallion in Perthshire; at Ballochbuie at the foot of Lochnagar in Deeside, Aberdeenshire; and at Rothiemurchus on the north-east slopes of the Cairngorm range, Inverness-shire.

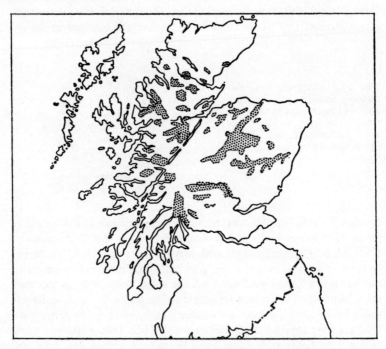

Generalised map of the native pinewoods of the Scottish Highlands. (Herbert L. Edlin of the Forestry Commission.)

CHAPTER 12

CONIFER PLANTATIONS

PINES, spruces and larches, because they are easy to grow and develop quickly into saleable timber on quite poor soils, are far more in favour among foresters than broad-leaved trees are. In the eighteenth and nineteenth centuries they were planted on quite a big scale in Britain by private landowners and were usually felled at the age of about seventy or eighty years. In this century when World War I had caused the cutting down of vast numbers of trees of all sorts, the Government decided on a large afforestation scheme in 1919 and established the Forestry Commission to carry it out. But only twenty years later there was another world war and by then the new plantations, though extensive, were not old enough to help the war effort very much. So further great inroads had to be made into existing older woods. Since World War II much has been done to replace those lost woods by further plantings by the Forestry Commission and by private owners. These new conifer forests are scattered throughout the country but most of the very big ones are in Highland Britain.

When the Forestry Commission began its work in 1919 the conifers chosen were the common natural trees of the Continent because it was assumed that such species would be the best for Britain; so there was much planting of European larch, Norway spruce (the Christmas tree) and Scots pine. But many of these plantations did not yield the volume of timber that similar plantations can produce on the Continent; and since those early days it has become accepted that these European conifers do not grow as well in the cooler, moister climate of Britain with its treacherous spring frosts as they do in the Continental climate with its harsher winters but more reliable springs and warmer summers. Eventually experiments with conifers from elsewhere suggested that species from the west coast of North America which has a climate similar to Britain's might thrive better. This seems to be especially true of the Sitka spruce which is planted mainly on the wet acid moorlands that cover so much of Highland Britain. It is like a very prickly Christmas tree and has needles which are green above and bluish on the underside. It grows quickly, has few pests or diseases, stands up to frost, wetness, low fertility and gales extremely well and produces a timber suitable for its commonest use – as pulp for the paper industry.

Obviously if you plant a moorland with trees you are going to alter its ecology and therefore the wildlife almost completely. To see what actually happens let us look at afforestation stage by stage.

First of all you put a fence round the area to keep out grazing animals; once you do that changes can happen very quickly. For instance, simply putting up a row of fencing posts across a patch of rushes can attract birds like whinchats because the males like to have a perch to sing from and so proclaim their territorial ambitions. Having set up your posts you complete the fence and shut out all grazing animals. Even if you never planted any trees the effects of your fence would be striking. Outside, the vegetation would be cropped short and would be preferred by those few birds such as wheatear, lapwing and golden plover which like to have some short turf in their habitat. But inside the fence there would be many more birds, small mammals and insects attracted by the deep growth of grasses, heather, bilberry, crowberry, gorse and other plants which would provide plenty of cover and food. Even if the ground is ploughed before afforestation, the eventual result can be much the same. After the young trees are planted the wild vegetation springs up again and provides suitable conditions (with little conifers as welcome perches) for meadow pipits, skylarks, tree pipits, grasshopper warblers, cuckoos and red grouse. In wet places birds such as curlew, snipe, dunlin and redshank may benefit from being protected by the forest fence. For the time being the whole plantation is much richer in wildlife than the moorland it replaced.

The growth of all this vegetation greatly favours the short-tailed vole – the commonest small rodent of uplands (it is found up to 1,200 m. on the Cairngorms), so much so that occasionally vole plagues have occurred especially after a succession of mild winters. The voles multiply until there may be more than 2,000 per hectare. This excessive population of hungry animals nibbling and tunnelling everywhere has very bad effects on the habitat. Most other small creatures suffer from the disturbance, the natural vegetation may be eaten to shreds and the young conifers are damaged by having their bark nibbled at. A most dramatic effect of these plagues is the large number of short-eared owls which come to prey on the voles, their favourite diet. Such an abundance of food causes the owls to lay more eggs and rear more young than usual and even to raise two broods instead of their usual one. Not that all the young owls grow up successfully: foxes which have also been attracted by the vole plague find young owls a welcome change from so much vole meat, and many owl nests are raided. During a vole plague in

PLATE 19. Ecology of three woodland plants. *Above left,* ramsons usually demands a fairly rich, wet soil. *Right,* wood spurge will accept various types of soil but it needs to be in southern England. *Below,* herb Paris requires lime-rich, fertile ground.

PLATE 20. More plants of fertile woodlands. *Above left,* dog's mercury has greenish, petal-less flowers. Note the long spikes of the male flowers compared with the short female spikes. *Right,* yellow archangel is widespread in woods except those on poor soils. *Left,* hairy St John's wort grows mainly in woods on lime-rich ground.

Short-eared owl with vole. This normally scarce owl can become abundant during vole plagues in young conifer plantations on moorlands

Scotland a fox's earth had the remains of eight adult and sixty-eight young short-eared owls in it.

The end of such vole plagues is, it seems, always the same: suddenly, when the number of animals is right at its peak, there is a sharp decrease. Just as no one knows what causes the plague we are equally ignorant why there comes this crash in numbers. But some scientists believe that overcrowding produces great emotional stress among the voles and that this so upsets the way important glands work in their bodies as to cause a complete break-down in health. After the plague the number of voles left is usually very small and the vegetation soon recovers from the devastation it has suffered. Most of the owls and other predators of course disperse as soon as the vole numbers decline.

The wildlife of a plantation never stops changing from the day the trees are put in the ground to the day the last ones are felled. These changes are always of interest and it would take volumes and many experts to describe them all in detail. Because I have studied the change of birdlife in plantations I will give a short account of them, but it needs to be remembered that mammals, insects and all other creatures go through similar transformations as the plantation matures.

When the conifers begin to grow and become bushy, the young forest slowly changes from grassland dotted with little trees to grassland dominated by shrubbery. What happens? You now find that still more birds are attracted but you begin to lose a few too: skylarks, for instance, and pipits and whinchats which dislike thick cover. Short-eared owls also go at this stage because the voles are now too deeply hidden to be caught. The curlew, snipe, golden plover and dunlin also depart, their nesting bogs by now drained and overgrown with trees. The birds that are gained are bush-haunting kinds such as yellowhammers, linnets, whitethroats, willow warblers, robins, wrens and hedge sparrows. In some forests pheasants come in at this stage, and in Highland Britain black grouse are likely.

The plantation changes rapidly and in a few years the trees are up to three or four metres and have bushed out to form an almost impenetrable jungle that stifles other vegetation except along rides and firebreaks. This we can call the finch and thrush stage. Three finches are likely colonists now: the bullfinch, which likes really thick cover, and chaffinch and redpoll, which prefer to nest in rather more open sites. The redpoll particularly has increased with the spread of conifers. Both blackbird and song thrush also now become common in the plantations; and where conifers grow on mountainsides the ring ouzel, normally a nester among heathery rocks, sometimes builds in the conifers. Wood pigeons too begin to breed in the young trees, as do garden warblers, for they love all this dense greenery.

Meanwhile the forest is getting too thick for some of the earlier colonisers. Robins, yellowhammers, willow warblers and others, which like spaces between the bushes, now go off to look for more suitable plantations. So do the black grouse for they too prefer a wood where there is more freedom of movement.

In the next few years the forest and its birds change enormously. The trees shoot up to six or seven metres, the lower branches are lopped and later some of the trees are taken out. This causes an almost clean sweep of the small, undergrowth-loving birds which formed the majority of the forest's population. Now it is the turn of larger, tree-nesting birds such as jays, magpies and carrion crows. Only two small species are common in these taller plantations: goldcrest and coal tit, both typical conifer birds. The goldcrest usually hangs its cradle-like nest from an outer bough; the coal tit often builds in a hole in the ground at the foot of a tree. In Highland Britain the siskin usually begins to breed in the forest at this stage: like the goldcrest it builds its nest on an outer branch and is very hard to find. The trees continue to grow. More of them are removed and now there are wider spaces between all the trunks. There is a deepening carpet of needles underfoot, but no ground layer, field layer nor shrub layer. Singing birds are very few and even in spring these older forests can be almost silent. By the time the forest reaches this nearly mature stage the jays and magpies have decreased for they have moved away to the thicker cover of younger plantations. But the final colonists now arrive, birds such as kestrel, sparrow hawk and the tawny and long-eared owls and, in Highland Britain, buzzards and ravens. By now the trees are producing cones and plenty of seed and become attractive to birds which have learnt to live on conifer seed in winter. In Scotland the crossbill may begin to breed in such plantations.

Because they are so important to the timber industry conifers have been intensively studied and foresters know where to plant the different species to get the best results. Far less is known about what long-term effects these conifers will have on the quality of the soil. It is sometimes said that, by their deep mat of needles and dark shadows, spruces cause deterioration of the soil and that broad-leaved trees with their more fertile leaf mould ought to be grown among the conifers to counteract these bad effects. But on the other hand there are spruce forests on the Continent that have presumably existed since the Ice Age and still produce fine trees.

Three kinds of larch are grown: the European, now right out of favour because it is subject to disease; the Japanese, which had a big

Japanese larch, usually seen in extensive plantations, grows quickly and has attractive reddish twigs conspicuous in winter

vogue but after about twenty years does not grow as fast as foresters would like; and the quick-growing hybrid larch, an accidental cross between these two, and grown particularly in Scotland where it originated. Larchwoods are very different from other conifer plantations. Their foliage is not nearly as dense as spruce or pine; the trees need to grow more widely spaced; above all they are deciduous. The result is that far more light gets into a larchwood than into other conifer woods and this means more plant-life, more insects, animals and birds. Moreover the larch, especially the Japanese larch, is a most decorative tree all the year, brilliantly green in early spring, beautifully yellow in autumn and red all the winter from the colour of its twigs.

Of other conifers in Britain the Sitka spruce is now by far the most commonly planted especially in the heavy rainfall areas of Highland

Sitka spruce, the conifer most commonly planted on moorlands, comes from western North America

Douglas fir, from western North America, grows fast in rich lowland soils and produces the tallest trees in Britain

Britain, for it needs more than forty inches of rain a year. Norway spruce, distinguished by its less prickly, all-green leaves is also widely grown. Scots pine is planted in many parts of Britain particularly in Scotland, but there are big plantations of it at Thetford Chase, East Anglia, Cannock Chase, Staffordshire, and in the far south of England in the New Forest, Hampshire. When we see how well pine grows if planted in the south of England we may suspect that its northward retreat in the Atlantic Period was not because it preferred a colder climate but because it was forced out of the south by the oak which proved more vigorous than pine in the warmer, wetter conditions.

Another pine now widely grown, especially on wet, peaty moorlands, is the lodgepole which, like Sitka spruce, is native in western America from California up to Alaska. Red Indians formerly used this pine's straight trunk to support their lodges or wigwams. From the same part of America comes the Douglas fir, named after the botanist who introduced it to this country. The tallest trees in Britain, approaching sixty metres, are Douglas firs. In America this fir grows to over seventy-five metres.

Yet other conifers from the west of North America which are used fairly extensively are western hemlock, grand fir and western red cedar.

PLATE 21. Plants of northern pinewoods. Both the twinflower (*Linnaea borealis, above*) and the one-flowered wintergreen (*Moneses uniflora, below left*) are rare. The chickweed wintergreen (*Trientalis europaea, right*) is much more widespread, being found locally in much of Scotland, parts of north England and also in East Anglia.

PLATE 22. Early spring flowers. Some woodland plants bloom before the trees shade the woods with their leaves. Typical are the lesser celandine (*above*) with its bright golden flowers, and the wood anemone (*below*) whose white flowers are especially characteristic of oak-hazel coppice.

Many other conifers are planted as individual trees for the sake of their beauty but few are grown as woodlands. There is however at Leighton, near Welshpool, North Wales, a famous grove of redwoods, another conifer from western North America. This magnificent wood which now belongs to the Royal Forestry Society is over 100 years old and contains a bigger volume of timber for its area than any other British wood. The soil, of course, is very fertile.

As for insects harmful to conifer plantations, these are many, but in British forests they have not so far proved disastrous. Most of the moths and beetles I mentioned as living on the native pines of Scotland are also found on pines wherever they are planted. A few more could be added to the list. There are, for instance, two fascinating wood wasps: the greater and lesser horntails. Three or four cm. long, the females of these formidable-looking flies use their strong, sharp ovipositors to lay their eggs in the living or dead wood of conifers, one egg in each boring. The larvae live by eating and tunnelling through the wood. In this arduous way of life they are aided remarkably by a microscopic fungus which the female horntail carries in her ovipositor and injects into the boring along with each egg. The fungus

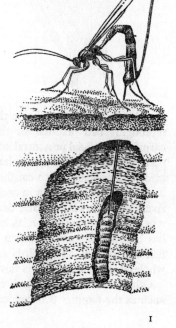

Rhyssa persuasoria, our largest ich-neumon fly, laying an egg in a larva of the giant wood wasp (or horntail) inside a conifer branch

immediately gets to work on the wood and softens it up, enabling the caterpillar to eat it more easily. Hidden in the wood these larvae are even there not safe from predators. Woodpeckers can find them. So can a large ichneumon fly, *Rhyssa persuasoria*, which detects them by smell and has as good an ovipositor as the horntail has. With this she penetrates the wood and lays her egg close to the body of the horntail larva. The larva which hatches from her egg then eats the horntail larva.

Rare but slowly increasing in pinewoods of the south of England is a big, grey moth, the pine hawk, which you might be lucky enough to spot clinging to the trunk of a pine in May, June, July. As common as the pine hawk moth is rare, is the pine looper moth which occasionally reaches plague numbers and defoliates the trees. To kill these little caterpillars foresters have sometimes sprayed the poison D.D.T. from

Pine looper, a moth whose larvae are very destructive of pine leaves

aeroplanes. But many people think that this spraying of D.D.T. is a thoroughly bad practice for three reasons. First, it kills *all* insects, harmful, beneficial or neutral and has resulted in serious infestations of pests whose natural enemies have been wiped out. Second, it poisons birds and animals which eat the insects. Third, some of the poison is washed off the trees by rain and eventually drains out of the forest into rivers and the sea, causing death all the way. In the United States where the spraying of forests has been done on a very big scale, there has been widespread pollution of rivers leading to the death of many fish and of fish-eating birds such as bald eagles and ospreys. Such wholesale use of D.D.T. is now banned in several countries.

Other insects which attack conifers include a few longhorn beetles such as the familiar two-banded longhorn, its long, dark body crossed

Two-banded long-horn (*Rhagium bifasciatum*) a common beetle whose larvae feed inside rotten wood, especially pine

by two pale-brown bars. This is no doubt a truly native species but some longhorn beetles, and wood wasps too, are thought to have been accidentally introduced in imported foreign timber. Some of them spend several years as larvae and pupae inside wood and though they start life in, say, a pine tree in Russia they may emerge as beetles or wood wasps from somebody's living-room door in Britain or elsewhere. Spruces suffer from various gall-forming insects. Aphids, for instance, make galls on the shoots, some of them resembling little cones; others cause the needles to grow curled up and deformed. Larvae of tiny moths, burrowing into shoots, cause them to bend over. The pine-cone bug hides in old cones during cold weather; in summer its larvae eat pine leaves. A well-known insect of pinewoods is the wood ant: it is

The wood ant is especially noticeable in pinewoods where it builds large mounds of needles

large, its vast multitudes can be heard as they scurry over the dry woodland floor, and they build mounds sometimes a metre or two in height usually composed of pine needles and little twigs. These large ants not only bite sharply but also squirt formic acid from their tail-ends in defence of their nest. Each nest contains a huge community of ants including several queens. There is no hostility towards neighbouring ant-hills because all belong to one huge ant colony. Many insects, notably small beetles, live as guests in these ant-hills: they give off a sweet juice which the ants enjoy, and in exchange the beetles are allowed to eat as many ant larvae as they like. Worker ants range far for caterpillars and seeds, and forage right up to the tree tops. In some German forests colonies of wood ants have been introduced, at a density of four colonies per hectare, to control insect pests.

People often comment on the effects that large blocks of conifer plantations have on scenery. Some like them, others do not. Naturalists are also divided in their feelings about the effects of alien conifers on nature. Some quite rightly point out that the great conifer plantations are a refuge for desirable animals such as deer, red squirrel, polecat, badger and pine marten, as well as birds like capercaillie, black grouse, siskin, crossbill and some of the rarer predators such as goshawks. But other naturalists complain that afforestation always involves the destruction of sites such as grasslands, heaths, bogs and streamsides, all of which are the habitats of many kinds of animals and plants. The losses are particularly great when an oakwood is felled to make way for conifers since, as I have said, oakwood can be our richest wildlife habitat. To be in an oakwood where all the birds are singing and the wildflowers are gay in the dappled sunlight of a spring day is a beautiful experience. Then if you walk from there into an adjacent mature spruce plantation you get the full impact of what a gloomy, flowerless, silent and depressing place a conifer forest can be.

But recently the idea has gained ground that Forestry Commission plantations, while keeping timber production as their main purpose, can also be used for pleasure. And since a lot of people who will visit forests are the sort who would get delight from seeing lots of flowers, birds and animals, it seems reasonable to hope that the forestry plantations of the future may be planned to cater directly for wildlife. The blanketing effect of endless spreads of conifers could be counteracted by planting them in smaller groups; establishing broad-leaved trees among them as individuals or groves; making pools in the forest; removing some of the conifers from the edges of lakes and streams in order to admit sunshine and warmth and so encourage more aquatic life; preserving bogs and marshes as the habitat of rare insects and birds; and by encouraging wildflowers and butterflies by the creation of clearings and wide margins along forest roads. So would be created a fascinating variety of habitats and these would soon be occupied by many kinds of animals and plants which the spruce blanket had smothered out of existence. And it could all be done with only a little loss of timber output. Against that loss could be set the pleasure people of all ages would get from being in such a pleasant forest and learning a little about nature and woodland ecology.

CHAPTER 13

OTHER WOODLAND TREES

OAK, beech, birch, ash, alder, Scots pine and a selection of alien conifers: these form practically all the existing woodlands of Britain. But, especially in the deciduous woods, there are other trees scattered singly, in small groups or in sizeable groves. In this chapter I summarise these other species.

Sycamore. Thriving in a cool, moist climate, sycamore lives in the mountainside forests of south and central Europe, growing up to 1,575 m. on sunny slopes in the Alps. It nowhere forms pure forests but grows among ash and beech. Like most trees it grows best on deep, well-drained, rich soil but it is widely tolerant and will thrive in practically any soil except the very shallow or the waterlogged. In Britain it is an alien, not being introduced until after the end of the Middle Ages. But its value as a timber producer and as an ornamental

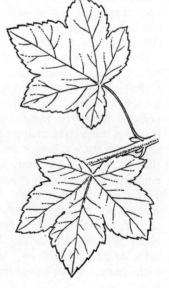

Leaves and winged seeds of sycamore. The wind-carried seeds help this alien tree to invade oak and other woodlands

tree have made it so popular that since the eighteenth century it has been planted throughout the British Isles; and because it is a vigorous coloniser it has spread itself into woods and hedges without any difficulty, its winged 'seeds' whirled everywhere by the gales of autumn. (A winged seed-case such as those of sycamore and ash, which does not open to release the seed, is known as a samara.)

There is no better illustration of the sycamore's thrusting powers than its success inside oakwoods. It has not only elbowed its way into the heart of these woods, it even establishes groves of its own within them. In fact some small former oakwoods have been completely turned into sycamore woods. How has it happened that the powerful oak has sometimes been driven to the wall? Probably the most important reason is that sycamore produces a crop of good seed every year whereas the acorn crop frequently fails. There is also the fact that acorns are evidently more palatable than sycamore seeds. They are also bigger and therefore easier for birds and animals to find. The result is that if a clearing is made in an oakwood, quite a thicket of young sycamores may shoot up from seeds that come winging in from a sycamore growing perhaps in a field outside the wood. For every twenty sycamore seedlings that spring up, there may be only one oak. Then, if grazing animals come along, they are likely to eat this single oak seedling but may take only the outside ones of a group of little sycamores. So a sycamore or two inside the group may survive to become trees. An oakwood clear-felled and then neglected can in this way become a pure sycamore wood, especially if the ground is nitrogen-rich, the condition most suited to sycamore.

Because it grows quickly and stands so well in gales, the sycamore has often been planted round exposed houses as windbreaks. It is the typical tree by upland farmouses in Wales, the north of England and the west of Ireland, no matter how high the houses are above sea-level, nor how close to the salt sea-spray. Where cow-manure from the farm buildings drains past their roots, sycamores really flourish for no site is richer in nitrogen. Except for birch and rowan it flourishes higher up British hills than any other broad-leaved tree, reaching 480 metres. Authorities differ widely about how long sycamores may live: some say 150, others say 600 years. Bee-keepers like sycamore because its scented, green, hanging flowers yield nectar freely in early spring. In fact, the trees when in flower really roar with bees, and not only honey bees but also mining bees and bumble bees, some of which work far into the dusk long after the honey bees have retired for the night (much to the bee-keeper's disgust!). Mammals and birds also like sycamore: mice and squirrels eat its seeds when they cannot get hazel nuts or acorns; finches, even crossbills, will eat sycamore seeds, and squirrels love to gnaw its sweet bark. (Sycamore belongs to the maple family which is famous for its sugary sap.) But rabbits are reported not to eat sycamore seedlings if they can find other food – another reason for its success as a coloniser.

Sycamore wood can be valuable if well grown and it is in some demand for slicing into the thin sheets called veneers which are extensively used for furniture. A variety of sycamore said to be found in Britain more commonly than anywhere else has an attractive ripple-mark in the grain and is much sought after by veneer makers. A large sycamore of this sort was sold in north Wales some years ago for over £1,000. It contained enough wood to cover an area equal to five football fields with veneer.

Aphids are abundant on sycamore foliage sucking at the tissues and then covering the surface of the leaves with the resultant sweet, sticky honey-dew which ants climb up to get. As we might expect in a tree that has been only four hundred years in Britain, not many caterpillars eat its leaves. The larvae of a few kinds of very small moths mine into or roll the leaves or live under the bark or in the seeds. Among larger moths whose caterpillars eat sycamore in preference to anything else are the plumed prominent, a rather uncommon species of south England, and the sycamore moth, commonest in south England and Ireland. Species which eat field maple may also be expected on sycamore as the two trees are closely related. A few gall-producers cause swellings on sycamore stems and leaves. Of attacking fungi, easily the best known is the tar-spot (*Rhytisma acerinum*) which puts large black spots on sycamore leaves almost everywhere in Britain. Exceptions are smoky districts of industrial towns where the fungus is defeated by the excessive sulphur dioxide in the air. As the air gets less foul by the introduction of smokeless zones it will be interesting to see whether the tar-spot fungus manages to re-invade these districts. What is mysterious is that a few country districts also manage to escape the tar-spot. For example in a mountain valley called Cwm Llwch on the north side of the Brecon Beacons in south Wales the sycamores are virtually free of the fungus, though no one knows why. Perhaps a fungus-resistant strain of sycamore grows in that valley. Experiments are being done to test this by taking seeds from the valley to see if the sycamores that develop from them will still be free from tar-spot when grown in other districts.

Hornbeam. Unlike sycamore, hornbeam is a native tree, having been in Britain since prehistory though it arrived later than most broad-

Leaves and fruit of hornbeam, a tree found most commonly in south-east England. Its seeds attract hawfinches

leaved trees and about the same time as beech. Widely planted in England and Wales, hornbeam is restricted as a native tree to southeast England and has a smaller natural range than any other tree. Britain's least known native forest tree, it is also the worst treated. The main reason for this is that its timber has always been disparaged. Though formerly used for cog wheels and pulley blocks it is too hard for most purposes, too unkind to the carpenter's tools, too difficult to work. Nor will it take a polish, so cabinet makers have never loved it. And as it springs up readily if cut down its main use in Britain has always been for poles: it has traditionally been part of the coppice along with hazel and birch. Or it has become a hedging plant for it makes perfect hedges which, like beech hedges, retain their russet dead leaves throughout the winter. But these are unworthy purposes for what can under the best conditions become a large and beautiful forest tree.

Not that hornbeam has ever made pure forest in Britain. Even on the Continent where it is often commonly scattered among other trees, hornbeam seldom makes pure forests except for a few in Germany and farther east. In Britain hornbeam is the natural companion of oak, either sessile or pedunculate. In Hertfordshire there are woods of sessile oak on sandy or gravelly ground with coppiced hornbeam dominating the shrub layer to the exclusion of hazel. In such woods the summer field layer is very sparse for hornbeam, like beech, casts a deep shade and suppresses all below it. Hornbeam is very common in Epping Forest where it has been ignominiously treated because of another of its properties – its remarkable heating power when burnt. So the villagers, exercising ancient lopping rights, always eagerly sought it for fuel and most old Epping hornbeams have been mutilated by pollarding.

Hornbeam seems to suffer from few pests in Britain, but its seeds, neatly equipped with a three-pointed wing as an aid to their distribution, are gladly accepted by wood mice and finches, especially the hawfinch which, like the hornbeam, is commonest in south-east England. As a planted tree hornbeam, though widespread in England and Wales, is rare in Scotland and Ireland. Fine specimens exist in large gardens, parks and arboreta for, given deep, moist, fertile ground, hornbeam

The hawfinch's strong jaws and beak are adapted to opening hard shells such as cherry stones

will grow as big as a beech. Foresters know this and always seem prepared to agree that hornbeam ought to be planted more than it is. But few of them ever seem to do it. A pity: for the hornbeam is a very attractive tree with a particularly beautiful, fluted grey trunk and bright autumn colours. Besides, with more hornbeams we would probably have more hawfinches.

Sweet chestnut. The sweet chestnut is so named because its fruit is the edible chestnut as distinct from the inedible conker of the horse chestnut. Sweet chestnut is also called Spanish chestnut but, though

Leaves and fruit of sweet chestnut. Introduced many centuries ago the chestnut is now widespread in British woodlands

common there, it is not more typical of Spain than other Mediterranean countries. In fact the chestnuts sold in our shops mostly come
from Italy where they grow much larger and ripen more readily than
they usually do in Britain. In south Europe chestnuts have long been
an important part of people's diet, but the tree is not considered a
native except in Asia Minor. It was probably obtained from there by
the Greeks who named it 'Kastanea' after a former town of that name
in Asia Minor. It was later taken over by the Romans who became
chestnut connoisseurs and spread it all over the rest of their Empire
including Britain. Whether they found it a disappointing cropper here
we do not know: but possibly in their time the climate was kinder and
allowed the chestnut to fruit more generously in Britain than it does
to-day.

But we must not be too contemptuous of our British chestnut trees.
They may miss the long growing season of the Mediterranean but the
nuts, though small, are fertile and produce plenty of natural regeneration. Not that we have any self-established chestnut woods: the few
woods of large chestnuts that do exist are all plantations. There is much
more chestnut coppice: it is mostly in south-east England and quite a
lot of it contains standard trees of oak or chestnut. In the woods where
the coppicing still goes on, the poles are cut about every twelve years,
a common use for them being as cleft stakes, for chestnut splits very
easily. The stakes are wired together to make an easily handled, quickly
erected, inexpensive type of fencing particularly useful for temporary
purposes. Chestnut wood can be mistaken for oak but seldom produces nearly such big beams or planks because, though it grows to a
huge tree, its timber is usually found to have cracks in it – a condition
which foresters call 'shakes'. Otherwise chestnut would probably be
grown on a much bigger scale for it grows quickly and will make very
big trees on poorer ground than is required by pedunculate oak and
therefore would not be in such competition with agriculture as oak so
often is.

Chestnut not only grows huge, it apparently lives to a very great age
and, having died at last, its hollow stump is said to last longer even than
oak. Britain's most impressive chestnut avenue is at Croft Castle,
Herefordshire. Our best known single chestnut is at Tortworth in
Gloucestershire. It was described by John Evelyn as a monster in 1706,
and is now a gnarled and hugely burred monster with great contorted
boughs growing out close to the ground. Most chestnuts achieve this
misshapen, writhing-in-agony look in extreme old age. But when
in their prime they stand very upright and tall, their trunks often grow-

ing with a pronounced spiral twist, some to the left, others to the right, a habit which produces the frequent 'shake' in the timber. Apart from a few bark beetles and a small moth whose caterpillar mines the leaves, the sweet chestnut is not particularly worried by insect enemies. Belonging to the oak and beech family, it is not at all related to horse chestnut, an introduction from the Balkans which regenerates freely but in our climate is evidently not thrusting enough to carve out a real place for itself in woodlands.

Yew. Although it is a conifer, yew does not bear cones. Instead it produces single large black seeds sitting in a fleshy red cup – a unique sort of berry that when abundant stands out conspicuously against the dark-green foliage. In all other respects yew is very conifer-like. Its

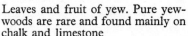
Leaves and fruit of yew. Pure yew-woods are rare and found mainly on chalk and limestone

berries are not true berries but were once cones whose scales, some time far back in evolution, fused together to become fleshy instead of woody.

Yew ranges widely in Europe from Scandinavia to the mountains of Spain, Sicily and Greece; it grows in the mountains of North Africa; in the east it spreads out of Europe far into Asia, reaching the west end of the Himalayas. Its pollen remains show it to have increased in Britain around 2000 BC and its wood has been found as charcoal on the hearths of Neolithic people. Yew has since then decreased all over the Continent where, though so widespread, it is now very local. And that is also its status in the British Isles: it occurs as single trees in many districts but as pure woodland it is scarce and nearly always on chalk or limestone (as it is also on the Continent).

In Britain the great yew country is where the South Downs cross the boundary between Sussex and Hampshire. Here are ancient yew groves tucked away at the heads of dry valleys folded into the chalky hillsides or growing along slopes in the lee of beechwoods: for yew, though as a planted tree it is often put in exposed sites, flourishes best out of the wind. At first sight these woods on the downs, scattered in little pockets, suggest the fragments of some vaster spread of yew that may have stretched far along the slopes, perhaps also the summits, of the downs. Maybe it did but, more likely, these downs were beech-covered until the beech was cleared away in the frantic search for fuel to feed the old Sussex iron furnaces. Then came the sheep and the rabbits which effectively prevented any beech regeneration. But yew is another story: yew foliage is distasteful, sometimes poisonous, to animals and yews can therefore easily hold their own while deciduous trees die out.

The best known of the South Downs yew woods grows in a deep coombe called Kingley Vale. Seven kilometres north-west of Chichester this lovely ancient wood, accepted as the finest yew wood in Europe, has views to the English Channel and to the Isle of Wight. In Kingley Vale (it is a National Nature Reserve but no entry permit is required) you can experience a quite unique sort of woodland, a wood of deep shadows that lie between the thick, grotesque shapes of what are, by far, Britain's oldest forest trees. For no British tree grows to the age of a yew: even oak and sweet chestnut probably do not get anywhere near it. But the age of the most ancient trees is difficult to say because they are nearly always hollow in the middle which prevents their annual rings from being counted when the tree is felled. A group of specially huge old yews at the bottom of Kingley Vale have been estimated to be 800-1,000 years old. Yews on the Continent have been put at two or three thousand years old. However, the world's oldest trees are the bristle-cone pines of North America; they have been proved to be 5,500 years old.

Yew is very tolerant of shade. Even under high beech forest, as on the Chilterns, where only saprophytes really flourish, the yew grows well except that there it cannot flower. But having so long a life before it the yew can afford to wait until a mere beechwood has had its day. Perhaps the yews of Kingley Vale also waited a few centuries under beech before they could form their own nearly pure woodland. It is not quite pure, however, for even there, on the outskirts of the yews, there are other calcicole trees and shrubs such as ash, whitebeam and juniper. Needless to say, on the deep, soft, densely shadowed carpet of yew leaves there is hardly any field layer or ground layer. Besides the yew groves on the South Downs there are also some on the North Downs in Surrey. Yews grow thickly too among the beechwoods that slope steeply to the Wye in the Blackcliff and Wyndcliff woods which together form a National Nature Reserve upriver from Chepstow, South Wales. In south-west Ireland yew grows as a thinly scattered understorey in sessile oakwoods near Killarney and forms at least one pure yew wood on limestone pavement there. Yew also flourishes in the New Forest, Hampshire, where it was often pollarded to get branches for yew bows, though the finest long bows were cut not from boughs but from trunks of yews.

Though wild yews grow mostly on ground rich in lime, yew when planted will grow almost anywhere, as you can see from the thousands which grow huge in country churchyards where they were presumably intended as a symbol of everlasting life. Probably the yew was already a sacred tree of the pre-Christian age. And since it is pretty certain that some of the first Christian churches were on sites of pagan worship it is reasonable to suppose that ancient yews stood on these sites already and that Christendom took them over as it did other symbols of paganism. If this is so, then some of our churchyard yews could be two thousand or more years old.

The poisonous properties of yew are due to a substance called taxine (from *taxus*, the Latin for yew). This poison is in the leaves, the bark and the seed. The leaves are eaten green by cattle without harm but are dangerous when dry and brown (most commonly in the form of hedge-clippings for yew is a favourite hedging plant). Birds digest the red flesh of the berries but the poisonous seeds come out in their droppings – in this way the yew is spread very widely. Few insects attack yews except a midge that often infects them heavily, causing large bud-like galls at the ends of the shoots. The few moth caterpillars that eat yew are mostly found more commonly on other trees.

Finally the name: while nearly all our woodland trees have Saxon names, yew is the only one that remembers pre-Saxon, indeed pre-Roman days. Its name is Celtic, like the modern Welsh name, yw.

Wych elm. Well grown in the open this can be a majestic tree: tall (up to 40 m.) with large yet graceful arching boughs often branching from near the ground. Found in most parts of the British Isles, it is less common in the south of England where it is scattered fairly thinly, mainly among the oakwoods. From the Midlands west into Wales and north into Scotland it is more abundant and is often locally dominant

Leaves and fruit of wych elm, a tree scattered through British woodlands especially in the west and north

along riversides – its favourite habitat. It also likes narrow valleys and even rocky gorges where it grows with ash, oak and small-leaved lime. Its soil preferences seem to be much like those of ash – mineral-rich ground, preferably but not necessarily with some lime, and with moisture moving steadily through the soil. Not surprisingly we find wych elm in plenty in those ashwoods on the limestone of the north and west. In such places it elbows the ash out completely here and there to form private groups of its own. In the days of wide-scale coppicing in the oakwoods, wych elm was seldom allowed the honour of showing what a fine tree it could be: oak was the preferred tree and wych elm usually got coppiced for poles along with hazel, ash and the rest, for it springs up readily after cutting. Apparently nowhere in its wide range across Europe and Asia does wych elm form large woods on its own: it prefers to insinuate itself among other species which it easily does, for its seeds, on round wings 2 cm. across, can carry far into the woods on the wind and germinate freely. In the deposits of the Atlantic Period a great deal of elm pollen is evident: this may have been predominantly wych elm but we cannot be sure of this because wych elm pollen is indistinguishable from that of common elm.

Man has planted quite a lot of wych elm on roadsides and in hedges for it is a very lovely tree particularly in April when it turns yellow-green all over with the fresh young seed-discs which appear before the leaves. Botanists who have studied genuinely wild wych elms have made the interesting discovery that their leaves, which are long and narrow in north and west Britain, get broader and rounder as you get towards south-east England. When a plant (or animal) alters gradually like this from one edge of its range to the other the series of changes is known as a cline.

For the insects found on wych elm see under common elm.

Common elm. If wych elm is the more characteristic elm of Highland Britain the common elm is the elm of the lowlands of eastern, central and southern England (and also of southern Ireland). In shape

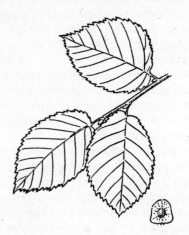

Leaves and fruit of common elm, a characteristic tree of hedges and roadsides

the two elms are very different. Whereas the wych elm is fountain-shaped, its boughs spraying out from a short thick trunk, the common elm usually has a trunk that goes up straight and tall, dividing much higher than the wych elm does. Then the common elm's boughs, instead of arching, often tend to go steeply up or at least hold themselves fairly level. The trunk is frequently clothed with a fuzz of short, level branches not much bigger than large twigs. Another difference is that wych elm leaves are usually bigger, rougher and narrower in proportion than those of common elm.

Common elm, because it stands tall and solitary in the hedges of thousands of fields is the most conspicuous tree of a great part of the English lowland landscape. Many villages, country churches and rural cricket grounds would look bare without their elms. Yet, though so common the elm is seldom in woods, a fact which has suggested to some people that it is not a native tree in Britain but was introduced by man. John Aubrey, for instance, in the seventeenth century wrote: 'I never did see an elme that grew spontaneously in a wood as oakes, ashes, beeches etc. which consideration made me reflect that they are exotique; but by whom were they brought into this island?' However, in recent times, botanists who have examined our common elm in detail find that it is not quite like those of anywhere else in the world and so must be native here.

Perhaps in the warmer climate of certain periods in prehistory, as during the Bronze Age, the common elm seeded itself easily in Britain. But now our climate seems too severe for it because though it blooms profusely, its reddish flowers gloriously colouring its bare twigs, they come too early (January-February) and get frosted in most years. The result is that common elm seldom produces fertile seed in Britain. It has overcome this difficulty to some extent by sending up shoots (suckers) from its roots and, since the roots of elms reach far just under the surface, it sometimes happens that an elm will surround itself with a thicket of little elms growing from its roots. Not often, however, for farm animals and deer are extremely fond of elm leaves and rarely allow elm suckers to develop.

But it is different with suckers protected inside hedges. Elm has in the past been valued highly for its wood, but because oak and beech grow so much better in woods than elm does, man has planted elm along the hedgerows where its suckers have spread in a long line on either side of it and helped to thicken the hedge. Elm, growing tall without big lower boughs, allows plenty of light under it and so is kind to the hedge below. But oak (or beech even worse) are not so good as standard trees in a hedge, smothering what is below. Next time you look at a hedge notice how often there are gaps below the oaks where the farmer has had to put fencing because the hedge has failed there. (All the same, the stock farmer likes to have occasional oaks in a hedge or in mid-field because their spreading branches give good shelter for cattle both from winter gales and summer heat.) Churchyards are a favoured locality for planting elms and in some districts they are commoner there than yews, growing to huge size because they are not felled for timber. Eventually they rot inside and often the top or a bough breaks off, creating splendid nesting sites for churchyard owls. Besides common elm several other very closely related elms are recognised by botanists as being peculiar to certain districts such as Cornwall, the Midlands and East Anglia. Most of them appear to be restricted to the British Isles.

Elm's most notorious insect is the elm bark beetle (*Scolytus scolytus*). Like other bark beetles, this species – it is reddish-brown about 6 mm. long – lives on the starches and sugars it finds under the bark. If you peel a sheet of bark off a dead elm you can nearly

PLATE 23. Common woodland toadstools. *Above,* from the two outside specimens flies have not yet removed the stinkhorn's slimy cap, source of the bad smell for which this fungus is notorious. The centre one, having lost its cap, is without smell. *Below left,* the prickly cap (*Pholiota squarrosa*) is a yellow-brown, inedible toadstool fairly common at the bases of broad-leaved trees. *Right,* the verdigris toadstool is one of the few fungi that are green. It is widespread in fields as well as woods.

PLATE 24. Enemies of the beech and other trees. *Above,* the bracket fungus, *Ganoderma applanatum,* is a common cause of heart-rot in old trees. *Below,* the oyster mushroom (*Pleurotus ostreatus*), which is edible when young, is another attacker of old trees.

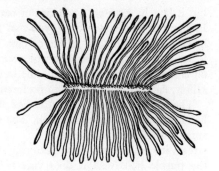

Galleries made by elm-bark beetle, carrier of the destructive Dutch elm disease

always find this beetle's characteristic parallel galleries. It is the carrier of a fungus called *Ceratocystis ulmi* which causes the very serious Dutch elm disease (so called because it almost wiped out the elms of Holland). This disease spread rapidly in Britain in the 1920s and many elms, including some fine old avenues, had to be destroyed. But eventually the disease slowed its advance and became merely local and by the 1960s foresters were talking about planting new strains of disease-resistant elms. Then in 1970 came what was to prove an even worse outbreak, elms being severely attacked in many southern counties of England and Wales. Though lots of them were felled to stop the disease from spreading, the method failed and in December 1972 it was decided to let the epidemic run its course. It is unlikely that anyone will again think of replanting elm on any scale until some way of controlling the beetle is available. Dutch elm disease is a problem not only in Europe but also in the United States and Canada. One suggestion is that the 1970 British outbreak originated in logs imported from America which were infected by a new and especially virulent type of the disease. As for explaining the association between elm-bark beetle and the fungus it carries, it may be that the beetles use the fungus to soften up the elm wood and make it digestible for their larvae. Some foresters believe that Dutch elm disease may always have been with us but that, for unknown reasons, it has not become extremely destructive until this century. Past outbreaks, being less virulent, could have gone unrecorded.

Of the larger moths those most nearly restricted to elm include the clouded magpie which is locally frequent in southern and western districts, including Ireland. In May and June you can find it sitting conspicuously about on bracken and any other sort of low vegetation,

w.   K

but it lays its eggs on wych elm or common elm. Mainly in southern England in July and August, you may find the caterpillars of the lime hawk-moth feeding on leaves of elm. Two reddish little moths, the lesser-spotted pinion and the white-spotted pinion, also lay their eggs on common elm or wych elm. The larva of another, the dusky-lemon sallow, eats wych elm seeds in preference to the leaves.

The caterpillars of two butterflies also eat elm leaves: white-letter hairstreak and large tortoiseshell. The white-letter hairstreak is a very small butterfly which is easily missed because, like the purple hairstreak, it spends much time fluttering high about tree tops. But unlike the purple hairstreak it does visit flowers, especially brambles, and that is when it can most easily be seen. The eggs are laid singly in July or August at the base of elm leaf buds and so they remain till next spring unless some long-tailed tit or other bird finds them. This hairstreak is fairly common in southern England, rare elsewhere. The large tortoiseshell winters as a butterfly in hollow trees and other hiding

Large tortoiseshell, a very local butterfly whose larvae feed on elm leaves

places. It lays its eggs in batches often near to the tops of the elms or at the ends of branches where its caterpillars, which remain in each other's company all their lives, may strip the leaves entirely off a small area. Perhaps you wonder why the large tortoiseshell lays its eggs on elm whereas its relations, peacock, red admiral, small tortoiseshell and painted lady lay theirs on nettles. But the difference between elm and nettle may not be all that great. Look them up in a botany book and you will find that they are placed next to each other in the classification of British plants; probably the chemistry and flavour of a nettle leaf have something in common with those of an elm leaf. But it may have been very far back in evolution that the large tortoiseshell diverged from the habits of its relatives, or the elms diverged from the nettles.

The large tortoiseshell is a magnificent butterfly but a rarity in most of Britain. It fluctuates a great deal in numbers, appearing for a season then disappearing for years, probably because it is highly susceptible to attack by ichneumon flies. Its stronghold is in East Anglia but even there it is quite undependable.

The wood of elm serves a variety of purposes from wheel-barrows to coffin boards. It stands dampness extremely well and centuries ago its trunks were hollowed out and used as water-mains. Many of the elm pipes which helped to supply London with water in the seventeenth century still exist underground, long since disused but still sound.

Willows. Included in willows are sallows and osier and in all there are nineteen British wild species. Some are restricted to mountains, particularly those of Scotland, and only a few are widespread. Willows generally like copious moisture and so are prominent in the shrub layer of damp or wet woodlands. Two species, the white willow and the crack willow, make large trees but, though common along rivers and canals, are seldom in woods except where there are streams or pools. Both are often pollarded. The pussy willow (*Salix capraea*) is less dependent on water and often grows in woods. Its male catkins, much visited by bees and other early-spring insects, are large, round and yellow and often called 'palm'. Common sallow (*Salix cinerea*) is another source of 'palm'. It is scattered in woodlands, and elsewhere it forms thickets in wet places, along railway banks and in many other habitats. There is also osier which has long, very narrow leaves and whippy twigs: it has been widely planted for basket and lobster-pot making, forms dense jungles in wet places but is no woodlander. Then there is the eared willow, a shrub mainly of sessile oakwoods, birchwoods and moorlands and commonest in Highland Britain and Ireland.

When a lake is silting up, willows are often an important stage in the succession. First the shallow water may be invaded by water horsetails, reeds and bulrushes. Then as the ground gets less watery little trees arrive, mostly willow and alder. For some years a willow thicket spreads everywhere but eventually the alder grows taller, suppresses the willow by its shade and we end with an alder carr.

As well as being beautiful, especially the kinds whose leaves blow white in the wind when their pale undersides are exposed, willows are of great interest to naturalists. Botanists study the various species and their many bewildering hybrids; and for the entomologist willows, particularly waterside willows, mean insects in abundance. Willow

Eyed hawk-moth larva on willow leaves

leaves are eaten by many species including about 120 kinds of caterpillars of the larger moths. They are also the food of the larvae of the purple emperor butterfly, in its few oakwood haunts in south England. These difficult-to-spot, pale-green, two-horned caterpillars feed mainly on the pale-green undersides of sallow leaves in April and May. The largest moth of willows is the eyed hawk; its voracious caterpillars often strip the leaves off whole sprays in late summer – a good clue to their presence except where saw-fly larvae have achieved the same result.

Among the other moths of willows is the puss whose large fantastic caterpillars, equipped with strange whip-tipped tails, also make a wholesale stripping of the leaves. The sallow kitten and the pebble prominent both have curiously shaped caterpillars that prefer willow to all else. The lunar hornet moth has a caterpillar which lives hidden inside willow or poplar twigs feeding on the pith. The clouded border is found wherever there are willows: its caterpillar is a little green looper abundant on the summer leaves. Another very common willow moth is the July highflyer whose caterpillar is remarkable for making tents of the fluffy white willow seeds in which it hides by day, coming out to feed by night. Though the larvae of one species of saw-fly eats the leaves in broad daylight fully exposed to view, several other willow saw-flies pass the larval stage hidden in galls – small swellings, some of them red, which are very abundant on willow leaves. These are known as bean galls. Other willow saw-flies make swellings on the stems or cause

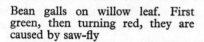

Bean galls on willow leaf. First green, then turning red, they are caused by saw-fly

the leaves to curl. Gall midges also produce leaf and twig galls on willows.

Many willows in the past have been pollarded to make them produce a regular crop of poles. The eventual result when cutting has long been abandoned, is a short thick trunk with a cluster of boughs growing from its top. Often rain gets into the crown of such maltreated trees causing them to rot inside and then become hollow. In this state they make the perfect habitat for countless species of beetles, moths and other insects. Birds as different as owls, tree creepers and mallard make their nests in these old pollards. Dead willow boughs that are soft inside are a favourite site for the burrows of leaf-cutting bees which line their mines with rows of egg-containing capsules each constructed of carefully cut out fragments of leaf.

Willows are quick colonisers of damp ground because their cottony seeds float in great quantities on the wind. A bird which makes particular use of these seeds is the lesser redpoll. Whenever she can get it, the female redpoll likes to line her little cup of a nest thickly with willow down and she will make quite long journeys to collect it.

Lime. Perhaps the first thing to learn about lime is that it has nothing to do with lime juice (which comes from a small type of lemon). The second is that most of the tall and stately limes which are so common in avenues, churchyards, large gardens, squares, parks and tree-lined streets are not the limes of our woodlands and so will not come into this book except to note that they are much disliked by motorists because if you park under a lime in summer you are liable to have your car covered with sticky honey-dew which rains down from the greenfly that infest the lime leaves in millions. Otherwise this is a popular and beautiful tree, very fragrant in July when in flower and very attractive to honey bees and other insects. It is not a native tree anywhere in the world but is a cross between two species (both British natives): the large-leaved lime and the small-leaved lime. The large-leaved need not concern us because as a wild tree it is decidedly rare in Britain. But the small-leaved lime is found scattered over England mainly between the Thames and the Humber. It is fairly frequent in parts of the Midlands and Wales and in one or two localities in the Lake District. It is virtually unknown in Scotland and Ireland and rare in England south of the Thames.

The peat formed in the Atlantic Period is so full of lime pollen that we must suppose that the small-leaved lime was a vastly commoner tree than it is to-day. Probably it never formed pure forests of its own but was abundant in the oak forests. As its wood has never been made much use of, not even as firewood, it has presumably been slowly eradicated from our woodlands by man and his animals. Perhaps it is most characteristic to-day as an occasional tree in woods on basic soils, often in shady, mild localities such as narrow valleys and streamsides. In some oak-ashwoods on limestone it can be quite a common tree. It is late getting its leaves and early in shedding them as if fearful of spring and autumn frost. At the northern edge of its British range (Lancashire for instance) its seeds seldom germinate in the wild.

Lime leaves are palatable to many animals: cattle, horses, sheep and deer browse on them avidly. So do insects: the larvae of beetles, sawflies and moths occasionally manage to defoliate a whole tree. The beautiful caterpillar of the lime hawk-moth is common in south-east England, including parks and gardens round London, where its food plant is frequently the hybrid lime. About forty species of larger moths have been found as caterpillars on lime. Several midges and mites commonly make galls on leaves and twigs of lime. Most spectacular are the bright-red nail galls that stand upright all over the upper surface of some leaves. Caused by a mite, they look rather alarming to lime-owners but apparently cause the trees no harm.

Poplar. In Britain we have three native poplars: aspen, grey poplar and black poplar. And several introductions which are far better known because often near or in towns: Lombardy poplar, white poplar, balsam poplar and black Italian poplar. Though they date back to prehistoric Britain none of our native poplars have won a conspicuous place in woodlands. Aspen is widespread in the British Isles but commonest in south-east England where it occurs in well spaced oakwoods. Grey poplar, far less common, is also found in damp oakwoods, chiefly in south and east England. It is virtually absent from Scotland and most

An ichneumon fly attacking a swallow prominent larva. Poplar is the food plant of this caterpillar

of north England. Black poplar (the genuine native as distinct from planted hybrids) is something of a rarity found in eastern and central England among wet-floored woodlands. All poplar leaves, highly nutritious and tasty to animals, are sought after by many insects including some seventy species of moths, best known being the poplar hawk, the commonest hawk-moth in Britain and found throughout the country. The black-spotted, yellow larva of the poplar saw-fly is often seen on the leaves which it eats and later on the trunk on which it pupates. Twigs and leaves of poplar carry many galls caused by beetles, aphids, midges and mites.

Cherries. Two kinds of cherry are frequent in the lower tree layer and the shrub layer of British woodlands. They are the wild cherry and the bird cherry, both outstandingly beautiful trees when in flower. The wild cherry (or gean) is widespread but is always most abundant in hedges and woods on the richer soils. It is especially characteristic of beechwoods on the Chilterns and of pedunculate oakwoods on lime-rich ground. In some parts of south-east England it is a big tree (33 m.) and takes its place in the highest canopy of the beechwoods, the timber of such splendid cherries being very valuable for furniture making. The red fruits are much smaller and fewer and usually less sweet than those of the cultivated cherry but are eagerly taken by birds. The white flowers of wild cherry hang along the boughs in loose clusters. Those of the bird cherry, also white, are in much longer clusters (racemes) and are held nearly upright or level more often than downwards. The bird cherry, usually a much smaller tree than the wild cherry, is mainly found in Norfolk, north England, Scotland and parts of Wales. It is rare as a wild tree in south England and Ireland. Its cherries are sour, pea-sized and black. Bird cherry is very hardy and recorded in Scottish woods up to 609 m.

Arbutus. In the mild, damp climate of south-west Ireland near Killarney, in stunted oakwoods growing on infertile soils, there is frequently a small tree called the arbutus or strawberry tree, a most

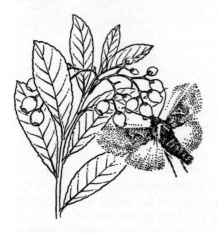

Silver-y moth at arbutus blossom. *Arbutus unedo* (strawberry tree) is native only in western Ireland where it grows very locally in oakwoods

interesting species because it belongs mainly to the western Mediterranean region. Several other species of the fauna and flora of western Ireland are also more typical of Spain and Portugal: they are known as Lusitanian species. (Lusitania was the name which the Romans used for Portugal and adjoining districts.) The arbutus has evergreen laurel-like leaves, clusters of small, creamy-white, bell-shaped flowers and strawberry-like fruits eagerly taken by birds though not by man. Its flowers are attractive to insects, particularly the migrant silver-y moth. It grows among the little oaks, being the same height as they are (about nine metres) but not under the oak trees for it is intolerant of shade.

CHAPTER 14

HEDGES AND SCRUB

HEDGES must be included in this book because they are, in fact, long thin lines of woodland. They are the home of many woodland insects, birds and mammals; and if a bank lies below the hedge there will be plenty of woodland flowers which, because of the good drainage and extra light, often grow better along hedge banks than inside woods. Sometimes, as well as a bank there is also a ditch and that too can be a haven for wildlife. Hedges have been well described as 'secret highways': they are not only places for plants and animals to settle in, they are also essential pathways along which countless species spread themselves out across the countryside linking one fragment of woodland with another so that the pattern of life that existed in the ancient forest cover is not entirely lost.

In areas of arable farming country where trees and woodlands are few, it is obvious that hedges are particularly vital to wildlife. Unfortunately in recent years farmers in those districts have been getting rid of more and more hedges because they want their fields to be bigger and because hedges are costly to maintain. So now nature conservationists are trying to persuade farmers who uproot hedges to see if there is somewhere on the farm a corner that could be made into a spinney or a copse where nature could survive. Just a few square metres of blackthorn, for instance, could be a nesting place for a thrush or a finch as well as a home for an intriguing, quite harmless, big brown moth called the lappet, and for two charming butterflies, the brown hairstreak and the much rarer black hairstreak (see page 43). Members of the British Trust for Conservation Volunteers are doing excellent work helping to create small wildlife habitats on farms where hedges have been removed.

Hedges, still so characteristic of much of the British lowland landscape, divide the farming country into a pleasing pattern of squares, oblongs and other less regular shapes. In all there are thousands of miles of hedges containing many kinds of shrubs and trees, for though hawthorn is the most common, you will find that every shrub that can make a hedge has been used somewhere or other. In a few districts, for instance, there are long stretches of hedge that are almost purely laburnum which make a marvellous show in June when they are hung with golden chains of blossom. In other districts the willow-leaved spiraea has been planted in hedges across wide reaches of country. In very mild districts you will see long hedges of fuchsia.

But these are exceptional hedging species, introduced from abroad, and generally it is the toughest natives that constitute our hedges, species which from earliest times farmers have been able to acquire and grow most easily. Which raises the question: how old are some of our hedges? This we do not know, but some hedges are believed to be over a thousand years old for they are mentioned in ancient records. There is an interesting theory about these old hedges: that the greater the variety of shrubs growing in them the older the hedges must be. This belief is based on the likely assumption that whoever first planted them used only one or two different species. Then once the hedges got established nature took a hand and very slowly other shrubs managed to get a foot in. So if you come upon a hedge consisting of say ten or a dozen different kinds of shrub you have probably found an ancient hedge. You could then try to confirm its age by consulting a local historian to see if, perhaps, the hedge is known to be an ancient boundary. This might well be a most fascinating bit of research.

What species of shrubs and small trees you may find along hedges depends very much on whether you are on lime-rich ground or not. If you are then the hedges are likely to contain maple, common buckthorn, guelder rose, dogwood, traveller's joy and sweetbriar; with the addition here and there of spindle, barberry and wayfaring tree. Away from chalk and limestone the hedge species are nearly always much fewer. But on practically all lowland farm soils, the commonest species are generally hawthorn, hazel, holly, bramble, elder, sallow, crab apple, blackthorn, field rose, downy rose, dog rose, honeysuckle and ivy.

No other habitat, except woodland margins, is so rich in shrub species as a hedge. And since most of these species are associated with special insects or other forms of life a hedge is clearly a first-class place to study animal and plant communities. Consider just two small examples from a vast number: they concern elder and wild rose. There must be something very peculiar about elder for not even rabbits will eat it; and on its bark grow quite a number of mosses rarely found anywhere else and also a strange-looking, velvety brown fungus called the jew's ear. On roses you will often find a fuzzy red gall several centimetres across called robin's pincushion. It is caused by a gall-wasp and is occupied most of the year by the larvae of this little wasp which lays her eggs in spring in leaf buds of the rose. As the gall grows so do the larvae inside it, but meanwhile it also gets invaded by the larvae's insect enemies as well as quite a crowd of harmless lodgers. In 800 of these galls an entomologist found a total of 24,000 insects, of which only a third belonged to the species of wasp which originally caused the gall.

The supreme hedging plant is hawthorn: cheap to buy, easily raised from seeds or cuttings, frost-hardy, wind-resistant, disease-free, long living, interlacing and prickly against stock and people, ever willing to spring up again when cut back and able to grow in almost any soil. But in well kept hedges man has reduced the hawthorn to a wretched state. So let us think of it as a tree, or rather as two trees, for there are two British species, one common, the other local. The common hawthorn is found all over the British Isles except for quite large areas of north

Left, common and *right,* Midland hawthorn. The common hawthorn has one pip in each berry, the Midland hawthorn usually two

Scotland which are without it. The other species, called the Midland hawthorn, is found chiefly in the east Midlands and south-east England but is absent from most of Wales, north England, Scotland and Ireland. Though it has been made some use of in hedges its chief habitat is the shrub layer of oakwoods particularly those on clay or loam. The leaves of the Midland hawthorn are less deeply lobed than those of common hawthorn, and the berries contain two pips (sometimes even three) instead of one. Both hawthorns take a long time to reach their full height of about ten metres and this slowness makes their wood very hard. In old age the trunk becomes gnarled and twisted and, when constantly rubbed by cattle, the bark becomes glossy and polished.

In its wild state, hawthorn occupies two distinct habitats: as part of the shrub layer of woods or as scrub. In woods of taller trees hawthorn is usually scattered rather thinly as if, unlike hazel for instance, it does not really like to be towered over by bigger trees. All the same it is widely found in all sorts of woods from sessile oaks on acid soils to the chalky slopes of the Chiltern escarpment. But it is as scrub that hawthorn comes into its own. On most types of soil, if a piece of grassland or other ground gets neglected, the birds will soon sow it with the ever-abundant hawthorn seeds; and though the young trees that spring up may have to struggle for a few years amongst a jungle of other plants, they will eventually grow tall enough to suppress them. So we get a natural plantation of young hawthorns. Then two things may happen if these little trees are left alone by man. Either they grow up into mature hawthorn scrub which may last very many years. Or, among the little hawthorns, the rooks or jays come and sow acorns which may, if rodents and grazing animals let them, grow up eventually into an oak-wood with hawthorn as the shrub layer.

When hawthorn forms scrub the trees grow close together, the leaves cast a deep shade and few shrubs or wildflowers grow below. But quite a few birds thrive in such thickets, attracted by the insects which feed on the hawthorn leaves and by the thorn-protected nesting places which the hawthorn offers. Perhaps the most characteristic nesting birds of tall hawthorn scrub are magpies: they build their great twig and clay nests at the tops of the trees and, as if the natural thorns all round were not enough, they add a dome of thorny twigs on the top. The berries of hawthorn usually last well into the winter as a vital source of food for blackbirds, redwings, fieldfares and waxwings; and

The waxwing, an irregular winter visitor from north-east Europe and northern Russia, lives on hawthorn and other berries

in a bumper year the berries are so vastly abundant that the birds do not nearly eat them all and the trees glow dark-red with berries as they catch the late-winter sunlight.

In hilly districts there is often a more scattered type of hawthorn scrub with plenty of open ground among the trees. This is when we see the hawthorn at its best. It has room to expand into a well-rounded shape and then in May or June covers itself all over with closely packed little white flowers which are highly scented and attract vast numbers of flying insects, among them honey bees, for hawthorn can be an important source of nectar for the bee-keeper. In the Highland Zone of Britain, hawthorn is characteristically scattered far up grassy slopes to as high as 600 metres. There it is a favourite site for carrion crows to build their nests which in later years may get used by merlins or long-eared owls.

Because it is so common and widespread and has palatable leaves, hawthorn is eaten by very many insects. Of the larger moths about eighty species eat it though, fortunately for the hawthorn, practically all of them eat other plants as well so that the trees are seldom stripped of their leaves except in a year when the pedunculate oaks are defoliated; then the hawthorn understorey often gets the same treatment, winter moth and mottled umber being the chief devourers. An interesting hawthorn moth is the Chinese character which, though mainly white, sits boldly on the leaves because its shape and pattern disguise it as a bird dropping. Another white moth, the yellow-tail, has the fascinating habit of laying its eggs on top of a hawthorn leaf then covering them with a bunch of hairs off the end of her body; the caterpillars that come from these eggs are evidently distasteful to birds because they are brightly coloured with red hair-tufts and feed conspicuously; their cocoons likewise are covered with irritating hairs – altogether a well-protected insect. Another hawthorn moth, interesting for a different reason, is the small eggar whose caterpillars live in crowds on webs slung conspicuously across the branches. What is curious is that the chrysalis, having tucked itself up into a tough brown cocoon, may stay in it several years (up to seven are recorded) before the moth emerges. Among other moth caterpillars which feed on hawthorn leaves are barred straw, mottled carpet, early thorn, feathered thorn, scalloped oak, swallow-tailed, brimstone and several emerald moths. The pale-green larvae of one of our biggest saw-flies also eats the leaves. The cocoons

Hawthorn saw-fly. Its oblong cocoons may be found in winter attached to hawthorn twigs

are brown oblong tubes attached to twigs and from them the hawthorn saw-fly whose wings are 3 cm. across, emerges by neatly cutting the cap off the cocoon.

In parts of Britain a special type of scrub is formed by juniper, our only native member of the cypress family. This evergreen shrub, which

Juniper either grows prostrate, as on mountains; or upright as on chalk downlands or in pine forests

on rare occasions grows into a tree ten metres tall, is commonest in the northern half of Scotland; but if we could look back a thousand years we would certainly find it was far more widespread then than it is now in England, Wales and Ireland. Outside Scotland, it survives only fragmentarily to-day, its chief localities being in north England, south-east England, north Wales and western Ireland. It is the same story all over Europe: in the clearance of land for agriculture and in the exploitation of forests, juniper scrub has been cleared away wholesale. Its world distribution is wide, extending from California across America, Europe and Asia as far as the Himalayas. In north Europe it grows up to the Arctic tundra; in the south, in the coolness of high mountains, it goes down into North Africa. In other words its climatic range is arctic and north temperate and it is the world's most widespread conifer. Its part in natural forests is no doubt important as a shelter for young trees of other species.

A tree does not become the world's most widespread conifer without being extremely adaptable. So although banished from more fertile ground juniper survives in places unwanted or neglected by man and we may find it on the windiest hillsides on the meanest soils. It has the advantage of being unattractive to browsing animals. But it has this disadvantage: being resinous (as you can smell from its foliage) it takes fire easily and it is fire that has probably removed it from many a stretch of common land and other former haunts.

One of juniper's best-known English habitats is in the south-east, on the chalk of the downs and the Chilterns where it spreads in black-looking thickets across the slopes. But at close range juniper foliage is full of subtle and ever varying shades of greys and greens and its reddish bark is often beautiful with silver-green lichens. The downs are lovely country for naturalists, because with the juniper is often a wealth of other chalk-loving shrubs such as wild privet, dogwood, common buckthorn, wayfaring tree and spindle as well as the traveller's joy that climbs and ramps all over the others, festooning them with white flowers in summer and grey feathery seeds in autumn. But, though beautiful, it is a powerful smotherer heartily detested by foresters when they see it in their young plantations.

How does juniper scrub manage to establish itself on the downs? It may begin when a patch of grassland gets overgrown by a few wild roses. Then in autumn redwings and blackbirds occasionally perch on these briars. The birds may have been feeding on juniper and hawthorn berries somewhere else and under the briars they leave droppings containing juniper and hawthorn seeds. The seedlings that come up next spring are not all eaten by rabbits, hares or sheep because these animals are mostly kept away by the sharp prickles of the roses. So, in the protection of the briars, a small group of junipers and hawthorns grows up. But they too are prickly, so as they get bigger and begin to bush out they keep the grazing animals farther and farther away, and so help other junipers and hawthorns to invade what was grassland. This colonising can continue until a whole hillside is quite dense with scrub. What sometimes happens then is that larger trees such as beech manage to get a place among the scrub and grow up to form tall woodland which overshadows the scrub and eventually crowds it out altogether, so completing a succession from grassland to forest. But in some places the beech has not succeeded in invading the downland scrub. Beech is not a rapid coloniser because its seeds are not usually wind-blown nor bird-carried and most of those which do happen to get into the scrub are no doubt quickly eaten by voles or mice. The result is that juniper and hawthorn scrub hold on to their hard-won positions along the downland slopes and have the permanent look of climax vegetation.

Ecologists, however, would tend to describe this sort of scrub as sub-climax vegetation.

When you see juniper so common on the chalk you might suppose it to be exclusively a lime-lover. But not at all. In north Wales, the Lake District and Scotland it grows in quite acid soils. It is at its best perhaps in Rothiemurchus Forest, Scotland, where in clearings in the Scots pines it makes big untidy clumps that are often three metres tall. It is common throughout the Scottish Highland woods not only in pine but birch. It is liable to be broken down by heavy snow – hence its sometimes dishevelled appearance. On the Scottish mountains it becomes a creeping dwarf. But up there in the company of purple saxifrage, mountain avens, least willow and holly fern we are getting a long way from woodlands. In several parts of Britain there are limestone districts (County Clare in western Ireland is an example) where juniper is common and permanent-looking, not just a stage towards woodland.

Juniper is peculiar in having two forms, one much less prickly than the other. The unprickly sort grows mainly on mountains and usually spreads itself over the rocks like a mat. The prickly sort grows in lowland districts and is the one that forms the downland scrub. As for the curious berries of juniper: these take two or three years to ripen, changing gradually from green to nearly black with a bluish bloom. So you can find them in all stages at any time.

Sometimes with juniper on the downs is a small evergreen tree called box. Its distribution in Britain is as narrow as juniper's is wide for it is apparently natural only in a handful of counties, all in south England. Locally it can be abundant, as it is at its most famous locality, Box Hill, on the escarpment of the North Downs in Surrey

Box, a small tree, probably native only on the chalk downs of south England

where it grows beautifully in the company of yew, juniper, whitebeam, dogwood, spindle and wayfaring tree. Near the top of the hill, box even grows in the shade of beeches, and because it stands shade so well it has often been planted in beechwoods as evergreen pheasant cover. So we must be careful not to assume that box is natural wherever we find it. Indeed some botanists have doubted if it is truly native anywhere in Britain. A wood so useful in carving, engraving and inlay-work, they claim, is very likely to have been introduced from the Continent. Box is a real lime-lover everywhere in its world range, which is mainly in south Europe and south Asia. It is particularly common on the lime-stones of central and southern France. In cultivation it is a well-known garden hedge and a favourite shrub for topiarists to fashion into fancy shapes. It has scented green flowers attractive to bees.

There are several other types of scrub. In some places there are whole hillsides yellow in spring with gorse, which is a favourite habitat of stonechats, yellowhammers and other small birds, by far the rarest being the Dartford warbler, a bird which can only just hold on to life in our coldest winters and so is restricted to the extreme south of England. In sand dunes another prickly shrub, sea buckthorn (no relation to our other buckthorns), can spread over wide areas with an impenetrable, silver-green jungle, smothering many smaller dune plants out of existence. Its one virtue is that its orange berries help to feed the winter thrushes. It is not the only dune scrub-former, for many dunes have great thickets of burnet rose, blackthorn, gorse and bramble. In inland places this sort of cover is often succeeded by wood-land. But normally there are very few trees growing near sand dunes and therefore it is probably unusual for tree seeds to get into dunes. Most that do are, no doubt, snapped up by rodents and those which survive cannot grow tall because they are incapable of tolerating the sea winds. So the only forests on sand dunes are those which are planted there and these are usually of pine, several species of which, particularly Corsican pine, grow very well in dunes because they are resistant to sea winds.

It will be seen that what most scrub-forming species have in common is prickliness – a necessary quality in the battle against animals. It is only where animals are few and where man is nearly absent that un-armed shrubs have any hope of establishing themselves. Such places are very rare in modern Britain but one of them is a great spread of almost bare limestone in western Ireland called the Burren. There, in what is virtually a rocky desert, an extensive spread of hazel has managed to develop. It is a remarkable sight for on limestone hazel is normally a mere shrub layer under ash. But on the Burren for some

W.   L reason, probably the prevalence of strong sea winds, ash has failed to get a hold. It grows in deep cracks in the rocks but hardly dares venture to poke its head more than a few inches above ground level.

Scrub is essentially an opportunist. It has to squeeze in where it can in a world where nearly all acres are precious. It may spring up anywhere, even in the middle of great towns, if a bit of ground goes derelict. In the countryside scrub is always appearing somewhere. A railway line is abandoned and in a few years we see scrub developing along it, a ribbon of briars, hawthorns and other shrubs stretching far through the countryside. Or an old canal goes dry or semi-dry and we get a different sort of scrub, maybe a long thin line of willows and alders winding through the land. Or hedges are neglected and swell out into thickets. Or whole pastures are abandoned as they have been in recent years on the Chiltern escarpment: they very soon turn into scrub, sometimes overwhelming rare orchids and other choice plants for which the chalk hills are renowned. So naturalists view scrub with mixed feelings. At its best it is the precious habitat of rare birds: the gorse which shelters the Dartford warbler for example. At its worst it is a smotherer of bee orchids and similar beauties of the downland turf. So people in charge of nature reserves have to be very careful about scrub. Some keep sheep out of their reserves so that scrub can grow up and provide cover for animals, birds and insects; others introduce sheep into their reserves to keep the scrub down and so allow wildflowers to thrive.

Hedges, on the other hand, are more universally welcome to the naturalist because they can be kept under control more easily. As one naturalist has put it, hedges form 'the largest area of nature reserve in the British Isles.' So every bit of hedge is precious, particularly in intensively cultivated districts where wildlife habitats are few. Nor do people have to be naturalists to appreciate this point. If they enjoy the song of the blackbird then they must place high value on hedges. For the prevalence of hedges in our countryside plays a great part in making this lovely songster Britain's most numerous bird. So if we want a symbol of the inestimable value of our hedges there it is – the rich chorus of countless blackbirds singing on a warm spring morning in Britain's countryside.

Woodland and hedges – such are the surviving fragments of the forests that were the background to practically all plant, animal and human life in Britain from the Old Stone Age to the Dark Ages. Then the forest got pushed ever more quickly into the background of most men's consciousness as farmlands spread wider and villages and towns grew up among them. Inevitably the woodland plants and animals shrank in numbers except those adaptable species which gladly came out of the woods to find a niche in the new man-created countryside. But they were a minority and the increasing spaces between the forests became chiefly a home for the kinds of plants and animals more typical of open country, whether they were hares, grasshoppers or skylarks. But these had to take second place to man, his crops and his domesticated stock.

In the woods it has always been different. Man may have often cut them down, replanted them and made great changes in them. Yet he has probably never lived in them but rather in clearings, and the bigger the better, for man has an inborn fear of the forest. As John Evelyn put it: 'It is natural for a man to feel an awful and religious terror when placed in the centre of a thick wood.' Certainly, European men are not now a woodland race. Some may work in the woods all their lives but at the end of each day they retreat to homes outside the woods. So the woodlands retain a feeling of ancient wildness that has gone from nearly all other lowland types of country. And with that wildness they have also kept much of their wildlife.

A woodland does not simply cover so much area of ground as grassland or heather moor does. It has another dimension – that of height. With its shrub layer and above that its tree layer it provides habitats at various levels up to the tops of its highest trees and we can observe how different forms of life have become adapted to these different levels. By catering for life in many layers one above the other, a woodland makes more use of the area it occupies than does any other plant community on land. In a healthy broad-leaved forest on fertile soil there is an impressive flow of life-giving substances always passing through it, through the great trees themselves, through all the lesser plants and through the bodies of every creature in the forest. All leaves fall to the ground at last, all plants and animals die. So constant renewal is always being brought to the forest soil, keeping it ever fertile.

Our woodlands survive as precious reminders of the forests of long ago. Though they have lost their larger animals such as bear, wolf, lynx, boar and in many places deer as well – aborigines of the truly wild forests – yet the woods still harbour many species from badger-size downwards. They also keep their ancient flora fairly intact. So they still have enough of wilderness atmosphere to make them interesting and refreshing places to visit. The conservation of woodlands, as well as hedges and some scrub, is therefore of importance: not only to naturalists but to all who value the existence of wildlife and wild and beautiful places.

English name:	Oak	Beech
Family	Fagaceae	Fagaceae
Genus	Quercus	Fagus
Species	1. robur 2. petraea	sylvatica
Meaning of specific name	1. Latin for oak 2. growing among rocks	growing in woods
Deciduous or evergreen	deciduous	deciduous
Type of leaf	alternate, simple	alternate, simple
Shape of leaf	1. very variable but generally rather oblong, deeply lobed with reflexed auricles at base; on very short stalk 2. less deeply lobed, base lacks auricles. On longer stalk	pointed, oval
Hairiness of leaf	1. usually no or few hairs 2. clusters of unbranched hairs on underside esp. where veins join midrib	hairs on leaf edge and veins of underside
Time of leafing (lowlands)	April	April
Time of leaf-fall	mid-Oct. to early Dec.	Oct.–Nov.; hedges and young trees may retain brown leaves all winter
Type of flower (both sexes on same tree in all six species except that occasionally ash and Scots pine have all male or all female flowers)	male: long hanging catkins female: short stiff spikes	male: hanging tassel-like catkins on long stalks female: on short erect spikes
Colour of flower	yellowish green	yellowish green
How pollinated	wind	wind
Time of flowering (lowlands)	May	April–May
Type of seed	single round nut (acorn) held in cup	1–2 triangular nuts enclosed in a case
Time of seed-fall	mainly mid-late Oct.	Sept.–Oct.

A TABLE OF FACTS ABOUT OUR COMMONEST NATIVE TREES

English name:	Oak	Beech
How most seeds are dispersed	birds and mammals	birds and mammals
Height reached in Britain	not usually over 27 m. but 40 m. is recorded	usually to 30 m., exceptionally to 40 m.
Girth reached in Britain (at 1 m. height)	occasionally 12 m.	6 m. not uncommon
Age reached	may remain sound nearly 300 years and linger for another 600	may remain sound 200 years
Type of roots	massive with deep tap-root	shallow
Age at which seeds are first produced	great variation in records but copious fruiting in British woods seems unusual under 50 years	about 60 years in woodlands
Typical soils in Britain	1. heavy basic clays and loams 2. mainly on well drained, acid soils and therefore often on hillsides of north and west	prefers mineral-rich soils on chalk and soft limestone in S. England and S. Wales; also on well-drained limeless soils
Fungus associations (mycorrhiza)	well developed	well developed
Altitudinal limit of British woods	300 m. but often lower in exposed sites (exceptionally to 430 m.)	305 m. (e.g. on Carboniferous Limestone near Buxton, Derbyshire)
Distribution of natural British woods	1. chiefly Midlands and south 2. chiefly west and north. But both species widespread and common except N. Scotland	Chilterns, Thames valley, Weald, Cotswolds and S.E. Wales
Frequency of good seed years	very erratic and local; perhaps on average a fair crop every 3/4 years and a heavy crop every 6/7 years	every 4/5 years on average

Birch	Alder	Ash	Scots Pine
Betulaceae	Betulaceae	Oleaceae	Pinaceae
Betula	Alnus	Fraxinus	Pinus
1. verrucosa 2. pubescens	glutinosa	excelsior	sylvestris
1. rugged 2. downy	sticky	very tall	growing wild
deciduous	deciduous	deciduous	evergreen
alternate, simple	alternate, simple	opposite, pinnate	needle-like in pairs
1. very pointed, ± ovate, toothed, some teeth larger than others 2. less pointed, ± ovate, teeth more or less equal	broadly oval, toothed	leaflets toothed, lanceolate or oval	linear, usually 30–80 mm. long (sometimes 100 mm.), 1–2 mm. wide, often twisted
1. hairless 2. usually downy, at least on veins beneath	hairless except for tufts in angles of veins underneath	hairless	hairless
April–May	April	May–early June	May–July
Oct.–Dec.	Oct.–Nov. after first frosts (leaves fall green)	Oct.–early Nov. Leaves fall green except that they may yellow in a dry autumn	leaves persist 2–4 years; most fall July–autumn
male: hanging catkins female: erect catkins	male: hanging catkins female: oval erect catkins	a much-branched inflorescence usually consisting of male and female flowers	male: catkins arranged in spirals round base of young shoots female: a cone
male: light-green changing to red-brown female: green becoming tinged with red	male: green or purplish female: dark crimson	purplish	male: yellow female: red-purple
wind	wind	wind	wind
April–May	March before leaves	April–May	May–June
very small with wings, one-seeded	very small with wings, one-seeded	a one-seeded samara	a winged seed, up to c. 40 per cone
Sept.–Nov.	Oct.–Nov. after first frosts or not till following spring	Sept.–spring (most seeds lie on ground 2 winters before germinating)	any time when cones are dry and open but especially in summer

A TABLE OF FACTS ABOUT OUR COMMONEST NATIVE TREES

Birch	Alder	Ash	Scots Pine
wind and possibly birds and small rodents	wind, water and possibly birds and small rodents	wind, birds and mammals	wind, water, animals and birds
1. 25 m. 2. 20 m.	12 m. average, sometimes up to 24 m.	not usually over 30 m., sometimes up to 43 m.	usually not over 30 m. (46 m. recorded)
up to 1.8 m.	up to 3.4 m.	up to 3.6 m.	up to 3.3 m.
80 years at least	c. 120 years max. but only c. 25 years on poor soils	200–300 years	nearly 400 years
shallow	adaptable, roots shallow or deep according to water table	deep-rooted wherever possible	sometimes shallow-rooted, sometimes with tap-root
7 years (even earlier under nursery conditions)	c. 30 years	30–40 years	seed as early as 6 years is recorded
1. light acid soils, especially sands 2. similar but more tolerant of wet and cold; therefore commoner on peaty moors	mainly on damp or wet rich soils; less vigorous on acid peat	base-rich soils and limestone	native Scottish woods are on lime-free, well-drained gravels, sands and clays deposited by ice or water
well developed	present but not strongly developed	apparently absent	well developed
600 m. in Scotland	540 m.	mainly lowland but up to 450 m. near Brecon	625 m. (Cairngorms)
widespread in Britain, commonest in Scottish Highlands	commonest in mixed woods; often forms small pure groves but large woods are infrequent. Pure alderwoods are best known on the Norfolk Broads	mainly in oak-ash woods in S. Britain but forms pure woods on mountain limestones in north and west	chiefly Deeside and Speyside (i.e. where climate is less oceanic than N. and W. Scotland)
abundant most years	abundant most years but these days alder no longer sets good seed above 300 m.	abundant most years	some seed most years but abundant only every 4–6 years

BIBLIOGRAPHY

Beaufoy, S. and E. M. (1953), *Butterflies of the Wood*

Blamey, M., Fitter, R. and Fitter, A. (1974), *The Wild Flowers of Britain and Northern Europe*

Burnett, J. H. Ed. (1964), *The Vegetation of Scotland*

Burton, J. (1968), *The Oxford Book of Insects*

Chinery, M. (1973), *Field Guide to the Insects of Britain and Northern Europe*

Chrystal, R. N. (1948), *Insects of British Woodlands*

Clapham, A. R., Tutin, T. G. and Warburg, E. F. (1962), *Flora of the British Isles*

Darling, F. F. and Boyd, J. M. (1969), *The Highlands and Islands*

Darlington, A. (1972), *The World of a Tree*

Edlin, H. L. (1956), *Trees, Woods and Man*

Edlin, H. L. (1958), *The Living Forest*

Ford, E. B. (1945), *Butterflies*

Ford, E. B. (1955), *Moths*

Forestry Commission issues reports, bulletins, leaflets, guides, etc., on many aspects of woodland management, wildlife and recreation

Hadfield, M. (1960), *British Trees*

Hickin, N. E. (1971), *The Natural History of an English Forest* (Wyre Forest)

Hoskins, W. G. (1967), *Fieldwork in Local History* (informative on the history of hedges)

Hyde, H. A. (1961), *Welsh Timber Trees*

Imms, A. D. (1947), *Insect Natural History*

Köstler, J. (1956), *Silviculture*

Laidlaw, W. B. R. (1961), *Guide to British Hardwoods*

Lange, M. and Hora, F. B. (1963), *Collins Guide to Mushrooms and Toadstools*

Longfield, C. (1949), *The Dragonflies of the British Isles*

Mandahl-Barth, G. (1966), *Woodland Life* (ed. A. Darlington)

Matthews, L. Harrison (1952), *British Mammals*

McClintock, D. and Fitter, R. S. R. (1955), *The Pocket Guide to Wild Flowers*

Mitchell, A. (1974), *Field Guide to the Trees of Britain and Northern Europe*

Neal, E. G. (1949), *The Badger*

Neal, E. G. (1960), *Woodland Ecology*

Newman, L. Hugh (1948), *Butterfly Haunts*

Nicholson, E. M. (1957), *Britain's Nature Reserves*

Ovington, J. D. (1965), *Woodlands*

Page, F. J. Taylor Ed. (1957), *Field Guide to British Deer*

Quist, A. (1971), *Epping Forest*

Ramsbottom, J. (1953), *Mushrooms and Toadstools*

Rodgers, J. (1941), *The English Woodland*

Royal Forestry Society, *The Quarterly Journal of Forestry*

Sims, E. (1971), *Woodland Birds*

South, R. (1961), *The Moths of the British Isles*

Southern, H. N. Ed. (1964), *The Handbook of British Mammals*

Step, E. (1932), *Bees, Wasps, Ants and Allied Insects of the British Isles*

Tansley, A. G. (1965), *The British Islands and their Vegetation*

Tansley, A. G. (1968), *Britain's Green Mantle* (revised by M. C. F. Proctor)

Tubbs, C. R. (1969), *The New Forest*

Yapp, W. B. (1962), *Birds and Woods*

For detailed scientific studies of individual species of trees see *The Biological Flora of the British Isles* published in the *Journal of Ecology*, e.g. Maple, Vol. 32; Alder, Vol. 41; Oak, Vol. 47; Ash, Vol. 49 and Scots Pine, Vol. 56.

INDEX